BUSINESS AND
FINANCIAL MODELS

STRATEGIC SUCCESS SERIES

BUSINESS AND FINANCIAL MODELS

CLIVE MARSH

KoganPage

LONDON PHILADELPHIA NEW DELHI

First published in Great Britain and the United States in 2013 by Kogan Page Limited

120 Pentonville Road	1518 Walnut Street, Suite 1100	4737/23 Ansari Road
London N1 9JN	Philadelphia PA 19102	Daryaganj
United Kingdom	USA	New Delhi 110002
www.koganpage.com		India

© Clive Marsh 2013

The right of Clive Marsh to be identified as the author of this work has been asserted by him in accordance with the Copyright, Designs and Patents Act 1988.

ISBN   978 0 7494 6810 1
E-ISBN   978 0 7494 6827 9

British Library Cataloguing-in-Publication Data

A CIP record for this book is available from the British Library.

Library of Congress Cataloging-in-Publication Data

Marsh, Clive (Clive Mark Heath)
  Business and financial models / Clive Marsh.
    pages cm
    ISBN 978-0-7494-6810-1 – ISBN 978-0-7494-6827-9   1. Business
enterprises–Finance. 2. Business planning. I. Title.
  HG4026.M3646 2013
  658.1501–dc23
                                                          2012041100

Typeset by Graphicraft Limited, Hong Kong
Printed and bound in India by Replika Press Pvt Ltd

CONTENTS

ACKNOWLEDGEMENT

I would like to thank John Caswell and Sarah Gall of Group Partners for their valued contribution of Chapter 3 to this book.

Clive Marsh

INTRODUCTION

The purpose of business and financial models

A good business model should describe how an organization creates and provides real economic and social value. It is a tool that enables an executive team to experiment with different business ideas and scenarios and to predict outcomes in a safe low-risk environment. The actual process of constructing a business model is a part of strategy formation.

A financial model means different things to different people. For our purposes it involves the task of building a financial evaluation from a more abstract business model. Financial modelling enables hypotheses and scenarios to be translated into numbers.

Economic, business and financial modelling has been around for a long time. My own first hands-on experience was with Shell UK Exploration and Production in the 1970s where models were an essential tool to making sound business and investment decisions. Scenario planning and sensitivity analysis were highly developed. When Excel became available business models were used by smaller companies as a basic tool for the analysis of important business decisions. This type of modelling will project and analyse different business scenarios and test their sensitivity to changes in assumption values and other variable factors. It is used for investment decisions. However, before anything can be modelled a business needs a vision – a valuable idea. This needs to be developed at the very front end of business modelling and we shall be looking at the 'thinking' process and idea-capturing tools using techniques such as visual thinking and contextual analysis.

The purpose of this book is to explain the use of the above techniques and processes used in modelling.

Assumed knowledge

To get the best out of this book it is assumed that the reader will at least have some basic accounting and financial knowledge. It is not absolutely essential but it will help. For this reason I would recommend that this book is read in conjunction with *Financial Management for Non-Financial Managers* also published by Kogan Page. Several of the financial models developed in this text are applied to examples from *Financial Management for Non-Financial Managers* to enable cross-referencing if desired. It will also be useful if the reader has previously used Excel. It is not necessary to be an Excel expert user but some basic proficiency will help. You will, of course, need access to Excel in order to use the templates.

About the author

Clive Marsh has worked for Capgemini Ernst & Young, IBM UK, Shell and several niche consultancies where he became aware of the value of visual thinking. It was during his time with Shell that he was involved with economic, business and financial modelling including scenario planning and sensitivity analysis.

Clive's previous published books concern corporate financial management. He is also a regular contributor to financial and business journals. He currently works with the Chartered Banker Institute as Verifier of Professional Standards and Ethics and as a tutor. He has a Masters Degree in Strategic Financial Management from Kingston University London, Business School, is a Chartered Banker and Fellow of the Chartered Banker Institute, an Associate Chartered Accountant of the New Zealand Institute of Chartered Accountants and a Fellow of the Chartered Management Institute.

Online resources

The following templates accompany this book and are available from
www.koganpage.com/strategicsuccess

1 – Straight-line depreciation
2 – Reducing balance depreciation
3 – Reorder different levels of annual demand
4 – Aged debtor listing
5 – Baumol Model for optimal cash
6 – The Miller Orr Model
7 – Net Present Value
8 – Internal rate of return
9 – Weighted cost of capital
10 – DCF method of valuation
11 – Standard costing variances
12 – Balance sheet, P&L and ratios
13 – Calculation of a total float and free float

CHAPTER ONE

STAGES IN THE DEVELOPMENT OF A BUSINESS AND FINANCIAL MODEL

Scope

A business model can cover the entire business or just a small part of it. Models are used for whole economies or just single business processes. They help define strategy and drive value.

FIGURE 1.1   Defining the scope of a model within the hierarchy of models is a key first step

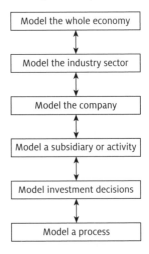

Defining the scope will help determine the fundamental question to be answered and the outputs required from the model.

In the case of an economic model the rate of inflation may be a required output whereas, in the case of a company model, inflation may simply be an item of input data.

This book on business and financial modelling is primarily concerned with modelling a company and its investment decisions. However, the techniques described can also be used and applied to other levels of modelling.

The fundamental question

Start by describing what it is that you want your model to tell you. Some examples of typical research questions are given below:

- What return will an investment provide under different business and economic environments?
- How will our existing business perform over the next five years?
- When is the right time to develop an oil field?
- What business should we be in?
- What is our future funding requirement and where should it come from?
- What is limiting our expansion?
- How sensitive are our profits to changes in oil prices?
- How do we manage risk and how can we diversify/spread uncertainty?

Note that these questions will typically ask what, how and when! They can be the final question or they might just be a subordinate question that requires an answer before the main question can be fully addressed. Once you have agreed your fundamental research question you can define the specific outputs that will answer it.

Think, what question would you like to address in your own organization? What specific outputs would you require?

Outputs

Outputs are what the model is required to produce to answer the basic question. The modeller must define these outputs at the outset. For example, in the case of a simple yes/no investment decision question the outputs may include the net present value, the return on capital employed, the internal rate of return, the pay back period and the discounted cash flow.

Inputs

Having defined the outputs it will now be necessary to define the inputs required to enter into the model to produce the outputs. This is the data that is required to feed the model in order to generate output and answer the fundamental question. A full definition of inputs may not be possible at the outset particularly in the case of a large model. Input recognition may occur during the operation and further development of the model. Typical inputs may include:

- Resources required. These will include:
  - Materials
  - Human assets
  - Overheads
  - Energy
  - Capital assets
  - Funding
- Skills, innovation and development
- Costings
- Customer information including:
  - Segmentation
  - Price sensitivity
  - Demand
  - Channels
- Competitor information including:
  - Barriers to entry
  - New entrants
  - Niche players
  - Market shares
  - Competitor supply costs
  - Competitor vulnerability
- Socio/economic factors
- Political factors including taxation
- Legal and regulatory

- Other variables including:
  - Inflation
  - Wage rates
  - Commodity and energy prices.

Defining limits to the scope of outputs and inputs can be difficult. Just how deep should you go? For example, would you just input inflation rates or would you input the variable factors that affect inflation rates? Define what you are modelling clearly. In summary, define your basic research question and output requirements first then research and obtain your input data required for your model.

The basic process is illustrated in the chart below:

FIGURE 1.2 Input – model – output

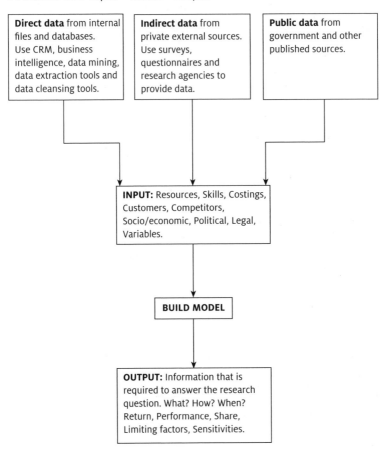

A step-by-step approach

There are no hard and fast rules governing the process of business model development. The chart outlined below is a guide and shows steps that may be taken and the information required.

FIGURE 1.3 Steps in model building

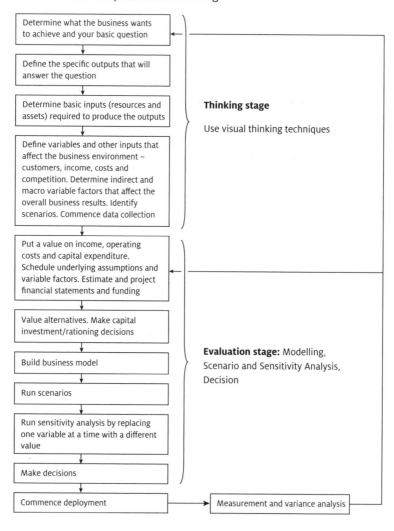

There are two initial stages in the modelling approach we shall use – thinking and evaluation.

Thinking

Thinking is all about making sure we are doing the right thing, or, ensuring that we don't do the wrong thing really well. To assist us with our thinking we can use visual techniques – in Chapter 3 Group Partners consultants explain how this critical stage works in practice. Since most strategic thinking is performed by a group (an executive team) this is best carried out in a workshop where ideas can be captured visually and where dialogue can be put into context. This will require a facilitator who is skilled in visual thinking and contextual analysis. Often the facilitator will be an external consultant, particularly if the organization is looking for new direction and is facing fresh challenges.

Our initial thinking process should reveal what we are trying to achieve and the measurable outputs. It will define the inputs and resources needed to achieve the required outputs and all of the variable factors that will affect outcomes. During this stage scenarios will be identified.

In the same way that we need structure to traditional business plans and processes we will also benefit from structure to our thinking processes. Thinking is key to all business and a structure to this process can enable more valuable thoughts to materialize and be captured.

Evaluation

The evaluation stage is concerned with understanding the financial consequences of following certain courses of action. This will include income, costs, capital expenditure, funding and evaluating alternative investment options. It will involve the building of a business model, scenario and sensitivity analysis. The evaluation stage should conclude with a decision.

Although I have shown the above steps in a logical sequence it is in fact an iterative process.

Skills required

You can, of course, prepare your own business model and this book is intended to enable you to do just that. Complexity is not necessary and is, in fact, dangerous. For example, some models become the play-things of those who enjoy introducing unnecessary complexity into their spreadsheets and this can lead to a lack of understanding and a cascade of errors. Essential facts may be misunderstood or go unnoticed. However, in larger organizations, where business and financial models concern large national/international-scale projects affected by many local and global factors, a broad knowledge and skill base may be required in the modelling team that supports the executive decision makers.

Modellers will require a knowledge of:

- Project management
- Workshop facilitation
- Visual thinking
- Contextual analysis
- The business and competitive environment
- The industry sector
- Data collection and management
- Marketing and sales
- Income and cost analysis
- Capital rationing
- Finance
- Taxation
- Human capital management
- Regulations and laws
- Strategy
- Discounted cash flow
- Socio/economic factors
- Environmental and sustainability factors
- Scenario planning
- Sensitivity analysis
- Spreadsheet preparation

This is a broad set of skills for one person to master and this is why business and financial modelling in larger organizations is usually carried out by a team. However, the team must be controlled and no member should become overindulgent in their own area of expertise at the expense of a loss of clarity for users of the model. Less is sometimes more and modellers should always take care not to introduce unnecessary complexity, inaccurate data or factors that have little impact on decision making.

It is usual to appoint an individual who will have overall control of the business model build project and its operation. This person will need project management skills in addition to a comprehensive knowledge of business and financial modelling. For the purpose of this book we will assume that you are the manager in overall charge of the model build, management and its operation.

Planning the model

A good business model is a sound investment. However, it is one that takes up a lot of valuable executive time and resources. In order to ensure that real value is obtained from the model it is essential that:

- the aims of the model are clear;
- the scope of the model is defined;
- there is a project plan to build the model.

Aims of a business model

You will need to give careful thought to what you actually want from your business and financial model. Typically, the aims will be some or all of the following:

- to define what a business should be doing;
- to describe how the business creates, protects and delivers value;
- to describe how opportunities can be realized;
- to identify the variable factors that effect the achievement of business goals;
- to establish how profits will be made;
- to understand risk;
- to enable business transformation.

At this stage it would be useful if you were to list what you actually wanted from your own business model.

Scope of the model

The scope of the model concerns how much of the business is to be modelled. Is it the entire business or is the scope to be confined to a part of the business or just a project? The scope is very much tied in to the basic research question, which can relate to the entire business or a part of it. For example:

- Where is an established business going over the next five years?
- Will an investment in a new oil field meet a required return on investment?
- How will a new business start-up perform?

Be absolutely clear of the business area you want to model.

A project plan to build the model

Once you have defined the aims and scope of the model you can develop a project plan to build the model. The ultimate goal of the project will be to build a model that will reach the aims and cover the scope of the model.

The project plan will identify:

- activities required to build the project;
- the duration of activities;
- the resources required to accomplish the activities;
- events that occur along the way such as the completion of key tasks.

Earliest and latest event times, float and the critical path are not usually critical for a small project such as this. Activities tend to run one after the other so the project can be plotted using a simple timeline table chart as on the following page.

FIGURE 1.4 Model build plan – tasks, resources and duration

Task	Manager	Duration (days)	Week 1	Week 2	Week 3	Week 4	Week 5
Visual thinking workshop. Research question and problem definition	CEO	3	3				
Definition of outputs	DOM	3	3				
Definition of inputs	COO	3		3			
Definition of variable factors; socio/economic, environmental, scenarios, sensitivities	CE	4		1	3		
Data collection	DQM	10			5	3	2
Value income, costs, capex, prepare financials	FD	3			2	1	
Evaluate alternatives, investment appraisal	FD	1				1	
Build model	MC	3				3	
Run scenarios and sensitivity analysis	MC	1					1
Make decisions	CEO & ET	2					2
Deployment plan	ET	2					2
Total time (work days)		35	6	4	10	8	7

Key:
CE	=	Chief Economist	DQM	=	Data Quality Manager
CEO	=	Chief Executive Officer	ET	=	Executive Team
COO	=	Chief Operating Officer	FD	=	Finance Director
DOM	=	Director of Marketing	MC	=	Model Controller

The roles listed above are just an indication of the skills needed by the modelling team. In a smaller organization you will find that they are carried out by fewer people. For example, the finance director may also act as economist, model controller and data collection/quality manager.

Keep things simple. The example of a project plan using Excel given in Appendix 2 is usually more than enough to control the build of a business model. Change the activities and durations to suit your own case. Get CEO sponsorship for the project and obtain sign-in from the team. Explain what is required and ensure they keep to the planned dates. Allow for some project slippage. If your company has a project management professional who uses one of the project management packages then of course you would use this resource. For large projects a Critical Path Analysis (CPA) and Gantt chart might be useful and these techniques are explained in Chapter 20. However, most small business models would be built before the team could be trained in the use of these techniques.

Data quality

It goes without saying that a model built using poor-quality data will at best produce unreliable results possibly leading to bad decisions. At worst it could be a disaster for the organization. Poor input equals unreliable and useless output.

Data collection commences once the inputs have been defined and may run throughout the duration of the project build. Clearly some activities cannot commence until data is collected. Data is continually refined and cleaned to ensure accuracy. A sensitivity analysis will indicate how sensitive the overall result is to an individual item of data.

Data sources may be external or internal. They may relate to public information or may require permission or payment to access. In the case of internal data the collection may require the use of data mining, extraction and cleansing tools. For example, large retail banks may use business intelligence software to collect data on customer behaviour and activities.

The length of time required to collect data will vary enormously depending upon the business. Where it is necessary to collect primary data there may be a need to construct questionnaires and brief a research firm. Some data may be very expensive to collect and may be unreliable. The model controller should be able to input several values into the model to test how sensitive the final result actually is to a particular item of data. He/she may decide that an item of data is of little significance to the final result and may not waste time and money collecting it.

Financial accounting, which is inherently focused on past performance and data that is of a quality to stand up to financial audit, provides good quality data. However, other data can be unreliable. Information from management accounts that are integrated with financial accounts is generally reliable.

Two main questions on the input concern the creation of snapshots in time to represent the state of the business (a moment in time that has real meaning) and devising consistency checks to cross-check the different parts of a data set. This is non-trivial in reality because data consolidations take place over time periods in real businesses, so 'a snapshot' can be difficult to create.

It is when you look at leading indicators of future performance such as how your employees feel and how your customers feel that you get into all sorts of woolly data, which may or may not be of good quality and may or may not be correlated statistically with the outcome you are trying to measure. If you are in this domain then the problem of determining if your data (usually collected for one purpose) is fit for the completely new purpose can be a challenge. In this case the provenance, quality and relationship of the source data to the outcome you wish to construct need to be proven.

Tools

Visual thinking techniques are valuable tools for getting to the real research question in order to make sure you are modelling future business opportunities and not simply projecting the past. Excel is an excellent tool used by many for financial modelling and many larger organizations integrate Excel with a database. For example, some build applications with an Excel front-end and a SQL Server DB back-end. The tools that you use will largely depend upon what is available depending on the size of your organization. This book concerns generic business and financial modelling processes and I will use appropriate tools to help describe those processes. You may use other tools.

Summary

Describe the scope of your model first of all. This means starting with the research question and defining the basic outputs required. Then determine the inputs required, remembering that data quality is all-important. Build and run your model to give answers to various business cases and scenarios and run sensitivity analysis. Test the quality of the answers by examining the quality and importance of each line of data. Continually refine the model. Use all tools available at your disposal. These will include:

- visual thinking and contextual analysis – to avoid doing the wrong thing really well;
- data mining and extraction tools – to obtain internal data;
- data cleansing tools – to help improve accuracy of internal data collected;
- Excel – to build and run the business and financial aspects of the model.

Keep the process and tools simple and avoid any unnecessary complexity that might camouflage a poor model. Some users of Excel, when trying to minimize the manual intervention of data, link many sheets together thereby introducing a greater risk of errors being introduced at a low level cascading throughout the whole model. Getting the right balance between keeping things as simple as possible and using the full benefits of Excel is key.

Remember that there are different levels of modelling and that an output for one level of model could be an input for another.

Three basic levels of model are:

Whole economy and macroeconomic models that are built to forecast the whole economy of a country. They model the effect of a government's decisions on interest rates, exchange rates, the gross national product (GNP), inflation and other economic indicators. This type of output may be published and used by industry and business modellers as input data.

Industry models that are used for specific industries and economic sectors. They may be used by industry associations and analysts to forecast likely industry performance.

Company models that may relate to the total activities of a specific company and be a part of the company's strategic planning process or just relate to a particular activity or investment opportunity. They are prepared using special modelling software or just using Excel. In the case of company modelling there is an increasing overlap with sound corporate governance requirements and a use of software that is designed to assist in this regard.

Your model should be used to help develop strategy and should be aligned with strategy to drive value.

CHAPTER TWO

DEVELOPING THE RESEARCH QUESTION AND OUTPUT DEFINITION

The basic question

The first step is to define the basic question that you want answered and then list the outputs that are required to answer this question. This is a critical stage of model development that may require the involvement of the executive team for reasons discussed later. Get this step wrong and you will be heading off in the wrong direction!

How easy or hard this task will become will depend largely upon the scope you have defined in the previous chapter.

For example:

1 Should M Oil Company develop the XY Oil field to commence production in 2017?
2 In which source of energy should Z Capital plc invest to help supply UK energy demand in 2017?

Both of these are complex questions. At a first glance question 1 may appear to have a narrower scope than question 2. However, expected movements in all energy prices and demand will affect question 1 just as much as question 2. It is a matter of how deep the analysis is scoped to go.

If the M Oil Company already owns the XY Oil field and is in the business of oil production then it might feel that it is locked in to realizing a return from its existing asset. In this case it might take a narrower view and scope. Where you cut the scope and questioning is a matter of careful and experienced judgement as much as analysis.

Of course, the basic question should be aligned with an organization's objectives and mission. However, how accurate are these and when were they last reviewed?

Getting the question right is of fundamental importance. It will:

'Help you avoid doing the wrong thing really well.'

I have taken these words from Group Partners, a firm of consultants, whose thinking processes we shall describe in the next chapter. You can explore the Visual Thinking and other techniques developed by this company on their extensive and informative website and Wiki links. However, for now, they are words well worth remembering. It does not matter how good and refined a business model is, it will be useless if it is answering the wrong question. Time spent at this stage is as important as time spent planning a passage to cross an ocean.

I mentioned above that the basic model question should be aligned with an organization's mission. A company's vision and mission statements may be defined as:

Vision statements
Vision statements define an organization's purpose in terms of values and beliefs rather than bottom-line profit and performance measures. A vision statement expresses values and purpose giving direction to employees and clarity to customers and other stakeholders.

Mission statements
A mission statement is primarily intended for the internal use of the executive team, shareholders and employees and helps define an organization's goals and objectives.

Some established companies, anxious to 'turn out' a vision statement, might first of all produce a mission statement based upon existing and established goals and then define the human value of achieving and delivering those goals. This may tick a few boxes but is hardly a close examination of a company's reason for existence or a basis for future direction.

The point here is that when defining the basic question for your business model make sure it is aligned to a vision and mission that is real and not just something that has been hanging on the wall for years. You may find that when defining a basic business model question you call into account the relevance of a long-established vision and mission statement. This is why the executive team need to be involved in this key stage of modelling.

Output definitions, examples, financial outputs

The outputs required from the model to answer the basic question need to be specifically defined. Examine the basic research question carefully and decide what information will answer it. This is best explained by means of an example.

Basic question:
Should a manufacturer of yachts invest in UK marina developments?

Outputs required to answer this question:
Expected return on marina development investments
Confidence levels
Revenue
Costs
Capex
Effect of diversification on existing business
Payback period
Estimated financial statements

Subordinate outputs that may be required:
Internal rate of return
Net present value
Cash flow
Demand for marina spaces
Market prices from competitors
Spaces available nationally
Risks
Future staff availability
Environmental risks
Planning acceptance confidence
Availability of sites
Need to include housing to make pay

Cost of ongoing dredging

Flood defence and Environment Agency requirements

Future oil prices and their affect on power boat usage

Funding costs and sources

The high-level outputs required to answer the basic question are simply: will the return on the investment meet the organization's requirements, when will this be achieved, how confident can we be of this happening, will it complement or detract from existing business and what effect will it have on funding/capital structure? The subordinated outputs are all the variables, costs, income, socio/economic and other factors that need to be taken into account to compute the value of the higher level outputs.

Clarity is needed to distinguish between outputs and inputs. For example, the net present value of a project may be considered an output. The interest rates used to determine the net present value in this case will be an input required to produce an output. However, in a macro-economic or high-level business model an interest rate prediction may be an output.

To produce some of the outputs listed above would require costs, prices, interest rates and exchange rates as inputs. However, you might consider these to be outputs. It will, of course, depend upon what you are modelling.

Lower level subordinate outputs and inputs will need to be quantified or coded in order to enter the business model.

As a rule of thumb, outputs are what you want and inputs are what you already have!

Outputs may be required to cover a number of years. A marina-type property development may forecast profits for a 20-year period. Forecasts of future periods will normally be expressed in real terms; that is, including the effect of estimated inflation on costs and prices. When using Excel spreadsheets for modelling it is normal practice to use the columns to represent the periods (years, quarters, months). You may decide to forecast monthly for 20 years in which case your sheet will have 240 period columns! Of course, you will consolidate this into 20 or even fewer columns for high-level and executive team presentations. Try and keep your use of Excel as simple as possible so that there is less potential for embedded errors.

Before getting too deep into model development the model builder should show the decision makers the expected outputs from the model and get agreement or amendment. At this stage it will be necessary to determine the units of measure. This is best presented in a simple table as shown below.

FIGURE 2.1 Output checklist for sign-off by decision makers

Marina development business model – output	Unit of measure
Key outputs	
Return on capital employed	%
Confidence levels	%
Revenue	£000s
Costs	£000s
Capital expenditure (CAPEX)	£000s
Effect on existing business	£000s
Payback period	Years
Estimated financial statements	£000s
Subordinate outputs	
Internal rate of return	%
Net present value	£000s
Cash flow	£000s
Demand for marina spaces	Number of boats
Market prices	£
Spaces available nationally	Number of spaces
Risks	£000s x p
Staff availability	Staff number v area
Environmental risks	£000s x p
Planning acceptance confidence level	%
Availability of suitable sites	Number of sites
Need to include housing in a marina development to make it pay	Number of houses
Cost of ongoing dredging	£000s
Flood defence and Environment Agency requirements	£000s
Future oil and diesel prices for boat users	$ barrel
Cost of funds	%

The ultimate decision makers will have to decide if the above outputs will answer the fundamental question, which is: 'Should they diversify their existing business of yacht manufacture into marina development?'

One of the main outputs mentioned above is estimated financial statements. Most business and financial models will require this and it is a must for a model for an entire company rather than just a single investment decision.

All organization business and financial models should have the following estimated financial statements:

- Balance sheet
- Profit and loss account (income statement)
- Cash flow statement.

You may also provide a source and application of funds statement.

If you don't have basic accounting knowledge then it is worthwhile taking a few hours out to get it. Of course, at this stage I would recommend my own book, also published by Kogan Page, titled *Financial Management for Non-Financial Managers*, 2012. Just read Chapters 3 and 4.

Balance sheet

The balance sheet is a statement of assets, liabilities and ownership (the amount the owners have invested on the company.

The profit and loss account (or income statement)

This shows the revenue, expenses (costs including depreciation) and profit (or loss).

Cash flow statement

This shows an estimate of the cash movements through the bank account – the cash received less the cash paid out.

Other outputs for financial modes

Some of the more common outputs that are provided by financial models are:

EBIT – Earnings before interest and taxation
NPV – Net present value
IRR – Internal rate of return
GP – Gross profit percentage
ROCE – Return on capital employed
EPS – Earnings per share
DY – Dividend yield
DC – Dividend cover

For the purpose of this text we shall use the most common ratios used as model outputs and I will now describe them below:

EBIT (Earnings before interest and taxation)

This is best explained by an example:

	£m
Sales	650
Cost of sales	300
Gross profit	350
Expenses	100
EBIT	250
Interest	30
EBT	220
Taxation	66
Profit after taxation	154
Dividends paid	40
Profit retained	114

The earnings before interest and taxation are £250m. Sometimes this will be referred to as profit before interest and taxation (PBIT).

FIGURE 2.2 Net present value (NPV) example

Year	Cash flow £	5% discount factor *	Present values £
0	−400,000	1.000	−400,000
1	+150,000	0.952	+142,800
2	+170,000	0.907	+154,190
3	+155,000	0.864	+133,920
Total			+30,910 (NPV)

*discount factors are provided in Appendix 3.

The net present value (NPV) is +£30,910. This shows that the project has a positive net present value after applying a discount rate of 5% p.a.

The formula for net present value is:

$$PV = \frac{FV}{(1 + r)^n}$$

Where:

> PV = Present value
> FV = Future value
> r = Discount rate
> n = The period

You can use this formula in your spreadsheet or use the discount rates given in Appendix 3. Alternatively you can set up a discount rate table on a spreadsheet.

Internal rate of return (IRR)

This is simply the discount rate that would discount a cash flow to give a zero net present value. It can be calculated by interpolation. Choose a discount rate that gives a cash flow a small positive value. Then choose another discount rate that gives a small negative value. Then the rate that gives a zero value must lie between these two rates and can be found by interpolating.

For example:

4% discount rate gives a NPV of +£17,150
5% discount rate gives a NPV of −£3,350

Then the IRR (the rate that gives a zero value) must lie between 4% and 5%.

A 1% move has resulted in a £20,500 change in NPV (£17,150+£3,350).

To move from +£17,150 to zero would require the following discount rate:

4% + (5%−4%) × (£17,150/£20,500)
= 4% + 0.837
IRR = 4.837%

Many analysts use the IRR. I often find that executive team members get confused with its meaning and for this reason I prefer to simply use the NPV.

Gross profit percentage (gross margin)

This is one of the most widely used and useful ratios. It is gross profit as a percentage of sales.

If gross profit was £350m and sales were £650m then the gross profit percentage would be:

$$\frac{350m}{650m}$$

$$54\%$$

Gross profit is sometimes called gross margin.

Return on capital employed (ROCE)

This ratio compares profits with capital employed to earn the profits.

$$ROCE = \frac{PBIT}{CE}$$

Where:

ROCE = Return on capital employed
PBIT = Profit before interest and taxation
CE = Capital employed

Earnings per share (EPS)

$$EPS = \frac{Net\ profit\ after\ tax}{Number\ of\ ordinary\ shares}$$

You can see that by defining the outputs first we are starting to identify the required inputs. For example, to provide the output of EPS we would need input data including the number of shares.

Inputs will be considered in a later chapter but for now you can see that a table showing input data against outputs can be completed once outputs have been agreed (see Figure 2.3).

FIGURE 2.3 Input data against outputs

Outputs	Input data required
Earnings per shares in £	Net profit after tax
	Number of ordinary shares
Net profit after tax	Revenue
	Cost of sales
	Expenses
	Depreciation
	Interest
	Taxation

Summary

In this chapter we have identified the importance of the fundamental question. This is a most important first step since getting it wrong will mean possibly doing the wrong thing well! To help get this question right and to identify the outputs that will enable the question to be answered it is useful to use visual thinking techniques for the team. We will discuss this in some depth in the next chapter.

We have described some of the more important and commonly used financial measure outputs together with subordinate outputs. These will enable the fundamental question to be answered. Defining outputs will enable the identification of inputs. Inputs will be described in more detail later.

CHAPTER THREE

VISUAL THINKING TO DEVELOP FUNDAMENTAL QUESTIONS

Contributors:
John Caswell and Sarah Gall

I feel that for universities and consultancies it is all too easy to become stuck with out-of-date business and financial modelling practices that have limited use in today's business environment. Perhaps there is too much emphasis on process and not enough thought given to fundamental questions. In the previous chapter I mentioned the importance of setting the right fundamental question and made reference to visual thinking as an aid. Group Partners are consultants in this field of 'thinking' and they have kindly contributed the following explanation of how they put this process to work. It is all too easy for a proficient business and financial modeller to 'get stuck in too soon' and end up doing an excellent job of solving the wrong problem. It is hoped that this contribution will help you avoid making this mistake – I think it makes valuable reading at this stage.

Clive Marsh

Challenging the traditional business model

The world has changed; therefore the business model has to change. And when the business model changes, everything encompassed by that business model has to change too.

The traditional 'process/method'-driven approaches of advisory and consulting practices evolved when the world was a very different place. These approaches worked at a time when the business could afford to follow fixed business models built around standard functional disciplines. That is not the world we inhabit today.

While the thinking behind the process has often been deep and rich it has been too singular in its focus. It was often designed to make the case for a certain (predefined) business model, technology or process. The world is now too dynamic and very different and the old approaches lack the agility required to cope; they have not evolved at the same pace. This has meant that the challenges to rethinking how problems get resolved and opportunity gets developed (and positively exploited) have changed dramatically.

While many organizations still struggle to articulate their needs in a manner that gives them the outcomes they really want, they are starting to appreciate that they can no longer continue to apply the old models or justify their excessive investment via external guidance – especially when that approach delivers such poor return.

New methods and approaches – a business model reflecting the world as it is today

At Group Partners we believe that these new methods and approaches are way overdue. We are passionate about working with businesses and organizations across the world to improve thinking about strategy, transformation and change – it's all about the business model.

Our way of working, using visual frameworks and other 21st-century tools, gets to the root causes of business problems and enables us to help our clients remodel their enterprise and create value from latent opportunities. It also avoids solving the wrong problem really well!

When we were clients ourselves we struggled to resolve complex issues just as our clients do now. It does not matter what their sector or geographical location is – whether they are publicly quoted or trustee run, whether they are huge multinationals or government departments – all of them face problems associated with complex 21st-century change. Just as they all have much greater opportunities that can be better engineered. But this degree of complexity and re-engineering can only be handled if the business model reflects the world as it is today.

Our methodology uses co-creation, visualization and logical structure applied to the important conversations in a business to transform the way it thinks and acts. And it does so quickly because this is the 21st century and we are using 21st-century tools.

Changing how you think about the future of your enterprise and therefore the business model is a big and increasingly essential step. Every leading business needs a distinguishing vision, a shared strategy and a meaningful roadmap of how to get there. It is not enough to stand idly by and watch as your competition innovates around you. You cannot ponder for too long over the changing dynamics of the 21st century. You have to act! You have to think differently about change.

It's always a leap of faith when transforming or changing anything. Reducing the risk during the change period is vital. Competition is intense and you need to be smart to survive – you need a new business model. Innovation and creativity in strategy are the key ingredients. Planning this future with your leadership team collaboratively and smartly is the only proven way to win because they more than anyone else need to understand the new business model and its potential implications on every part of the enterprise.

Structured Visual Thinking (a trademark of Group Partners): principles for a dynamic world

We have developed a philosophy we call Structured Visual Thinking™ (SVT™), a Dynamic Architecture™ that ensures we look at the whole picture – and that over time enables the client, with or without our help, to continue to develop and improve it – and an approach we call 4D™ during which we workshop particular issues in facilitated sessions with the client. This approach is the accumulation of 11 years' work, including almost 3,000 interventions with all kinds of businesses in every category, large and not so large, and with governments, NGOs and other not-for-profit organizations.

Change within the dynamics requires leadership with vision and courage

There will be no dynamic change in the business without the earlier creation of a new business model, a compelling vision and strategy. Today, nearly all business operations are structured according to how we have 'thought' about things. Their operational models, just like their business models, have become habits – habits that are hard to break. They have all the key elements – policies and procedures, an existing business model and a set of beliefs – core organizational values, a mission statement, and a set of goals.

However, vision and strategy alone, no matter how compelling the purpose, will not result in productive change – and certainly not change that makes a positive difference in how the enterprise actually needs to operate in a new and dynamic world. The business model – where the 'rubber hits the road' – is what will force a change in behaviours and the breaking of old habits.

Facilitating dynamic change – dynamically

It is now widely accepted that accelerated change and value creation is improved by impartial facilitation. Respectful facilitation along a sequence of well-understood processes is core to everything from peace talks and conflict resolution through to business transformation and strategy creation. In Structured Visual Thinking™ certain phases are more suited to intervention and other phases happen remotely, but each step relies on gathering, understanding and developing insight and data. Everything is in the pursuit of causing fresh dialogue for the development of new thinking and outcomes. SVT™ enables us to take a whole system view of all the moving parts and to position the new business model within the existing context.

We have observed that meaningful work is founded on three major planks:

● Visualization of the opportunity or desired change in live co-created interventions.

- Recognition of the complex patterns in data that when worked collaboratively and reflectively sets up better analysis and synthesis of what we know and therefore a new narrative.
- The creation of a complete 'diagram' of the enterprise shown as a living system so that people can see the machinery and how and where they fit in.

These foundational elements are how we work, how we think and what we do. We do not use visualization to over-simplify or to deflect but to signify logic and meaning and connect purpose with decision in a rapid way. Complex patterns are used to identify risk and opportunity and engage with practical, actionable work. We use systems thinking to engage, inform and empower the widest possible audience.

SVT™ enables us to:

- visualize critical information and future scenarios – in context – to ensure multiple stakeholder access;
- cause vital conversation – building consensus around logic and structure;
- synthesize large amounts of content and data within visual interfaces to ensure fast access and application;
- ensure sharp and effective communication through world-class visualization;
- demonstrate how change and transformation may look in the future;
- create clear and compelling stories about complex and often intangible business ideas;
- gain rapid alignment of the leadership team around the new business model, strategy and vision;
- make decision quality a standard through logic frameworks;
- build engagement and ownership throughout the enterprise via shared and meaningful artefacts.

Structured

Structure is critical for people within complex environments to create some kind of order within which to think, imagine and then construct new value or enhance decision making. In order to deploy a new business model we need to understand how to make new choices, and to make better choices we need to 'sort' in a more disciplined fashion.

Structure organizes the complexity of thought, idea, conversation, and – in our work – each important factor of strategy or transformation.

Structure is a broad-based understanding about how to organize a decision process, both in the small and in the large, to ensure adequate discovery of the relevant context, brilliant thinking about the range of possible solutions, sharp dialogue when it comes to making trade-offs and smart use of information.

Visual

We apply visual techniques because they accelerate meaning and purpose between people. We create things visually to convey understanding. The powerful symbols we design, develop and create for our clients enable better knowledge exchange. These visual 'objects' and scenarios are used either to provoke further conversation or to translate intangible ideas into physical systems and outcomes that can be shared, telling the new stories across the enterprise.

Organizations so overvalue words and impenetrable PowerPoint decks that they easily lose sight of the elegance and simplicity of visualization: to create context and persistence; to create the place and opportunity for sparking new thoughts, discovering unexpected juxtaposition. In some cases, the right way to do that is creating massive maps on walls 40 feet long. In other cases, a stack of index cards and some markers might be the right tool.

Thinking

Thinking is at the heart of everything a business needs to do. It is more important than ever because of the need to improve performance, create efficiencies, solve problems far more quickly and identify new value ahead of our competition. We are passionate about finding better ways to think; uncovering new value through collective and ever more coherent thinking. We want to leverage the talent and often-untapped creativity in everybody we work with.

Sharp thinking is a function of many things. We want to be sure that we bring the very best thinking we can, and put our thinkers in spots where they can be the very best possible versions of themselves. From a process standpoint this means bringing industrial-strength methods, frameworks, processes and tools to bear – the right ones given the nature of the problem – to ensure that the people working the problem do what is necessary and sufficient to work it in a high-quality way.

The Group Partners approach to the business model and strategic decision making

Group Partners believes there are only two really valuable things that we can do for business: solve the right problems or create value out of opportunity. Value is the additional premium we place on something; a quality that distinguishes it from other things and is worth paying (extra) for.

Value, however, often defies our ability to mine, define or control it. There are some great ironies and paradoxes in this and you're likely to need new skills and new ways of thinking if you're to go deep into why change is necessary.

New value from a new business model will only emerge:

1 If we're ready to have some deep and very fundamental conversations with ourselves.
2 If we can think sufficiently differently to understand why it isn't already there.
3 If we can use the new way of thinking to see how it can be created and sustained by the capability and resources currently within the enterprise.
4 If we can identify and prove who says that there is value in any of this anyway (customers).
5 And if we know what are the moving parts and dynamics (many of which are outside the business) that will need bringing under control if we are to make that value worth mining over time.

Doing this calls for unusual capabilities, ones that involve weaving patterns, painting visions, hunting fresh clues, distilling data, harvesting knowledge, writing and then telling the stories about new visions and business models – getting out into the world and gathering different ideas. All of these skills are fast becoming part of the new language of change and as yet are still scarce in the business world today. Without them, though, you're unlikely to be equipped to explore the new business model and the value in it. So you're going to need to change – some of the people, some of the processes – and gain different capabilities to ensure different behaviours.

Just saying that today's business world is complex is far too simplistic a way to put it. Today's world is where human nature translates as ingrained behaviour – new pressure from fast market entrants that are designed to eat your lunch meets outdated platforms and infrastructure and talent and scarce capability – they all add up to some pretty wicked issues that need tackling.

An architectural approach to building a future

In our world in order to create a new business model everything starts with the establishment of a Dynamic Architecture™ (see Figure 3.1) that is designed to imagine and then to reflect the 'DNA' of the organization. This architecture allows us to identify, consider and then reshape the business model and the way we go on to manage and plan our way through any change that is required. It connects all the 'moving parts' and maps the implications for the enterprise in terms of the way it needs to organize, manage and operate. Within this frame any necessary changes can be imagined and understood and a more adaptive and agile model developed.

It is often the case that change doesn't happen (at all or quickly enough) because the root cause of why it needed to change and what it needed to become wasn't identified. This Dynamic Architecture™ enables us to reduce the risk and improve the performance of how we align and equip the enterprise to take better advantage of the world in which it operates.

FIGURE 3.1 Group Partners Dynamic Architecture™

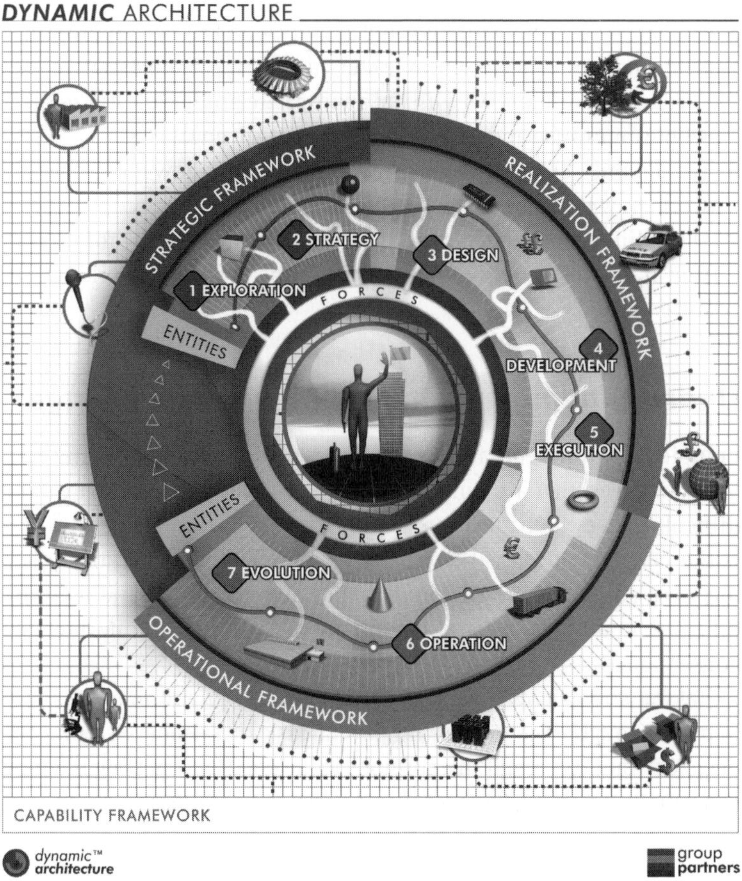

DYNAMIC ARCHITECTURE _____

CAPABILITY FRAMEWORK

dynamic™
architecture

group
partners

Group Partners Dynamic Architecture™ approach depends on:

1 Context – access to the widest possible context – data, insight and information.
2 Collaborative mindset – a collaborative frame of mind and the systems and tools in place to co-create with the business.
3 Commitment – enlightened leadership – working with the right people; people who care about the outcome.
4 Persistence – a dynamic enterprise strategy is not created by workshops; it is an attitude, a way of life. Our work begins when we start talking with the business and from minute one we are picking

up clues and starting to think about creating value or solving the problem.

5 Holistic – sustained thinking and activity with the right approach; from change agents to senior leadership and from collaborative systems and interviews with the appropriate groups and out to the whole enterprise and its stakeholders – all are engaged.

6 Leadership – clear messaging from the top about how it is going to work, how it will be sustained and managed.

7 Discipline – most organizations are not good at stopping things – this is a maturity of thinking and discipline. It is about working differently.

Understanding a dynamic blueprint for change

Complex environments are dynamic; they are influenced by many variables – 'forces' that are fluid and constantly evolving. While it can be difficult to see the patterns, these forces exist within a system – this is the business and it is these patterns and dynamics that make each business unique. There are forces that can be recognized and there are others that are invisible and potentially contain risk and unintended consequences.

Taking strategic decisions in these dynamic environments is perhaps the toughest and most important task of a leader. Getting the decision right can result in enormous value creation – getting it wrong can equally destroy value; and even destroy the enterprise.

Progress in dynamic environments can be difficult and even dangerous

Once the Dynamic Architecture™ is in place we design and then develop a structured engagement with the right people in the right context so that we can fully consider the opportunity or issue that is presented, construct a compelling vision and engineer a business model to deliver and sustain it.

Understanding the wider picture is vital if we are to avoid solving the wrong things and that means extending the capability to think and know it way beyond the competency of any individual – so this is most definitely a team sport calling for commitment, discipline and courage and above all enlightened leadership.

At this stage we introduce the tool we call 4D™. In one or, more likely, several 4D™ sessions with the client it allows us to gather all of the information required to understand the problem or opportunity properly and then to make effective choices about how to improve the situation. We look at the whole picture and then over time develop/ improve it – moving from the current state towards a future state.

4D™ approach

This approach delivers sustainable value. It has been proven over the long term to deal with every significant business issue.

The 4D™ process starts by describing 'where the future lies' within what we call an Exam Question – a statement of purpose written as a positive phrase that describes a clear intention for progress.

For the Exam Question to be answered properly we need to consider all the variables that are likely to cause pressures or barriers and also those that can be powerful allies and leverage-able. We then apply one or more of the 4D™ frameworks (in sequence), each requiring its own preparation and sometimes its own Exam Question.

Each framework is governed by a Business Equation, a 'forcing mechanism' that enables us to be sure of covering the ground in the way and in the depth needed to fully answer the Exam Question.

The equations for the first two 4D™ Frameworks follow. In each case the letters in brackets refer to the conversation/discussion or module that addresses this part of the equation. The order in which these modules are tackled may vary according to the specific circumstances of the assignment and the Exam Question governing it, but as a general rule the order below prevails.

D1 Business Equation: Discovery and Alignment

Which message or offer [H] about which blend of product [E] and service [F] [tangible and intangible assets], through which channel [D], addressing what trend or point of pain [C], to which most valuable customers [B], displaying what aspiration or need [A], built on which criteria [H] with what capabilities and behaviours [I], against what timeline [J] achieving the goals [K] at minimum risk and maximum return on investment?

D2 Business Equation: Development

To achieve the desired Strategic Outcome, or ultimate goal (H) and in order to experience the Redefined Conditions (G)... the effects that result in new value which is in turn underpinned by considered Governance, Capability and Cultural environment (Operating Model) (F), what is the planned Roadmap of Activities and Actions (E), (or Action Plan) that will deliver against the agreed significant Strategic Themes (D) that will drive the business towards the new Future Vision (C) based on the strategic Business Imperatives (B) (the business drivers) which will move the business away from the Current Reality (A)?

The Discovery Framework

Discovery (D1) is the first stage in Group Partners 4D™ approach to solving complex business problems. It is typically a full-day workshop during which we work with the client team to discover what we 'could do' to tackle the Exam Question.

Working through the 11 modules of the framework over the course of the session, we create alignment around the key stakeholders and uncover how far we agree and share common ground and definitions. The nature of the approach with its emphasis on collaboration and co-creation means that although there may initially be a divergence of views, by the end of the session we will have built out of the ideas and energies of those present a shared vision of what we could do.

This is high-energy, co-creative thinking that tests, aligns and forces the best possible outcomes using the underpinning Business Equation logic. This forcing equation – like its Development counterpart – explains the reasoning behind the construction of the framework and why we work through it in what may at first appear an unlikely order.

The modules allow us to cover the Exam Question from two directions. First, to identify how aligned the leaders are on their objectives, their assets and their marketplace (customers and wider stakeholder prioritization and insights). Second, to push hard at thinking through what needs to be done – scenarios of possibility for the future, potential value propositions, criteria for making smarter decisions, implications on the operation/business model, devising a roadmap that makes sense – if we are to change successfully.

The Development Framework

Development (D2) is a high-energy, co-creative intervention that starts to synthesize all we discovered in the Discovery phase if there has been one (there isn't always either the need or the time). If this is the first intervention, we will take what we have already uncovered in pre-intervention discussions with the client and from our own research and build on that. In either case, as we work through the framework's eight modules we will be starting to create strategies, change scenarios and hard plans for the future, effectively covering the three main questions anybody needs for a new business model:

1 Where are we going?
2 What, as things stand, is stopping us getting there?
3 How then are we going to get there?

Within these main aspects we cover strategic aims, objectives and outcomes, the metrics we expect or seek, the realities that are barriers or demand leverage, the vision we want to inspire people with, the imperatives, the strategic themes, the new operating model and the roadmap.

Where there are several areas of concern or if topics arise that people feel would benefit from a separate look, Development can be cycled a number of times (additional sessions do not necessarily need to follow on directly one from another). Such additional work frequently brings to the surface specific issues that deserve a closer focus, which is where our Deep Dive framework comes into its own.

Consolidation

By the end of D2, the client team have been enabled to see and better understand where there are gaps. They appreciate that more or simply better data is needed to fill the holes and go away armed with the tools to do this remotely by prioritizing between the many options of the strategy and feeding back the results to us. Armed with their feedback, we can begin building towards the communication of the result of this alignment and creativity.

It's worth stressing, however, that although this initial framework can be built within 2/3 days, preceded by appropriate preparation; full realization of the desired change requires the team to continue the work beyond the engagement (our support is of course readily available when/if needed).

The consolidation, communication and ongoing realization phases are where our Podio Collaboration Areas begin to come into their own. As soon as possible after a D2 session, we upload the visuals (first in hand-drawn, then in digital format) into a client-specific, fully protected space in the online work platform Podio so that everyone has access to what we have co-created, and for the team to share internally if that's been agreed as appropriate at this stage.

At this point, we can take the work further into the third 4D™ phase – Decision (D3) – which sorts all the choices into a coherent set and fleshes out the roadmap to take them forward.

The Decision Framework

Decision making is at the heart of 4D™. This is where we need the best possible data and rigour because it is where we place our bets. There are three main components to this D3 framework: The Outcome metrics and KPIs (Key Performance Indicators) we see; the strategic choices we have determined during Discovery and Development; and thirdly the roadmap, which defines what the client will continue doing as before, start doing differently and stop doing as a result.

The Deployment Framework

The fourth programme, Deployment (D4), rests on the real outcomes from the previous three 4D™ phases and as such builds from understanding the real requirements and not those that simply suit a predefined solution or product set. It can only properly begin once final approval presentations and sign-off from D3 have been given, teams built, a programme office put in place and timelines and expectations managed.

We support Deployment with any number of roadmaps, flight-plans and time-lined/milestoned events, responsibilities, actions and measures – and wherever appropriate will connect this phase directly to systems of workflow and programme management with alerts and dashboards.

Primarily, however, our job now is to help the team and others choose the right roads. Some may be clever short cuts to somewhere else, some pure dead ends and some may present big challenges but are the only way to get there. We have therefore created templates for the team – and often at this stage, wider stakeholders – to input the true milestones and 'journey signage' needed to implement the new business model and ensure that the new strategy reaches fruition.

This often involves working more widely with people, causing behaviours to change, encouraging adoption, improving leadership and so on but it also means clear, crisp, meaningful and coherent communication.

Outcomes and deliverables

The outcomes of our session work are captured to help the team after the event. Our capture is in no sense a verbatim note-taking exercise. It involves conscious choices about what to include and what to leave out. We listen for clues behind the conversation that can create an emotional connection that can be sustained after the workshop experience is over. Because the outcomes may be presented to people who were not at the session(s), we use our Visual Thinking techniques to ensure that the narrative is always meaningful and to convey in the most compelling way what we have learned and where it will go next. It is as much building a story as it is a record of the discussion.

These deliverables are appreciated and whatever form they take (executive summaries, framework context books, workbooks, interactive systems) we make sure they are rapidly available (some even in real time). We also ensure that they are augmented and/or in the correct form and with a degree of simplification that will enable them to be used widely by different stakeholders. In all instances, our aim is to make these tools as interactive as possible and highly engaging.

Summary

Group Partners has a vision for the 21st century. We want to change the way that business thinks and works and we want in all we do to avoid solving the wrong problem really well.

Against a constant tsunami of complexity, opinion and dogma we aim to achieve the quality of thinking that marks out the real leaders. Real leaders are wise and profound, they are the strategists, the 'imagineers'. They are designers, storytellers, artists – they are the definition of leadership. They actively encourage fresh input, new ideas. They will say when they are wrong – and remain cool when challenging the status quo. They challenge it with good reason because they are balanced – they are the positive disruptors. And they have humility, grace and charm even in the most harrowing of times. It's because they are constantly figuring out how a newer/better world would work that they retain this focus. To them fresh ideas are the raw material of everything humans currently do and might possibly achieve. Critical Thinking is the machinery that uncovers, inspires and encourages an 'idea' and turns it into valuable action. We call all of this creativity and it is what we excel at. It is what makes the difference.

I hope you have enjoyed reading this contribution from Group Partners. A key message for us business modellers is that we need to put at least as much effort into thinking and fundamental questions and that we need tools and a framework to help us do this.

Clive Marsh

CHAPTER FOUR

INPUT DEFINITION

Basics of input definition

Output and answers to the fundamental question can only come from input data. In this chapter we will show how inputs are identified.

Having identified the outputs required using the process described in Chapter 2 prepare a table identifying the inputs needed. Clues to this often come from the output description. Some examples are given in the table below.

FIGURE 4.1 Input identification

Output	Input required	Unit of measure
Profit before interest and taxation	Sales	£ / $ / €
	Cost of sales	£ / $ / €
	Expenses	£ / $ / €
	Depreciation	£ / $ / €
	Inflation	% p.a.
	Rates of exchange	£ / $ / €: Currency
Gross margin	Sales	£ / $ / €
	Cost of sales	£ / $ / €
Net profit	Profit before interest and tax	£ / $ / €
	Interest	£ / $ / €
	Taxation	£ / $ / €
Gross margin %	Gross margin	£ / $ / €
	Sales	£ / $ / €
Return on capital employed	Profit before interest and taxation	£ / $ / €
	Capital employed	£ / $ / €
Net present value	Future value of cash flow	£ / $ / €
	Discount rate	%
	Period	n=number of years
Payback period	Net investment	£ / $ / €
	Benefits (incremental sales)	£ / $ / €
Cash flow	Cash income	£ / $ / €
	Cash outflows	£ / $ / €
	Period	n=number of years
Capital employed	Ordinary shares	£ / $ / €
	Term loans	£ / $ / €
	Other sources of capital	£ / $ / €
Weighted average cost of capital	Cost of shares	% p.a.
	Cost of term loans	% p.a.
	Cost of other sources of capital	% p.a.
	Total capital	£ / $ / €

Schedule of inputs required

From the above example you can see that many of the outputs depend upon common input data. For example, the profit before interest and taxation output and the gross margin output both require sales as an item of input data. At this stage it is useful to prepare a table of the base-line data required:

FIGURE 4.2 Base line input data

Input required	Unit of measure
Sales	£ / $ / €
Cost of sales	£ / $ / €
Expenses	£ / $ / €
Depreciation	£ / $ / €
Inflation	% p.a.
Rates of exchange	£ / $ / €: Currency
Profit before interest and tax	£ / $ / €
Interest	£ / $ / €
Taxation	£ / $ / €
Gross margin	£ / $ / €
Capital employed	£ / $ / €
Future value of cash flow	£ / $ / €
Discount rate	%
Period	n = number of years
Net investment	£ / $ / €
Cash income	£ / $ / €
Cash outflows	£ / $ / €
Ordinary shares	£ / $ / €
Term loans	£ / $ / €
Other sources of capital	£ / $ / €
Cost of shares	% p.a.
Cost of term loans	% p.a.
Cost of other sources of capital	% p.a.
Total capital	£ / $ / €

The above table shows the base line data input that the outputs depend upon – the database. In the diagram below we can see how the common base data might serve outputs:

FIGURE 4.3 Input database and outputs

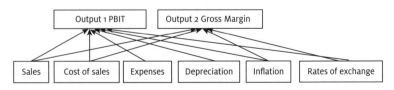

Schedule of formulae to derive outputs

To arrive at the value of outputs will require the application of formulae to the input data. Most modellers will use a spreadsheet. Examples are given below:

FIGURE 4.4 Calculation of GP, PBIT and GP%

	A	B	C	D	E
1	**Calculation of GP, PBIT and GP%**				
2					
3					
4	Sales		Input	60	
5	COS		Input	−20	
6	GP		Output	40	
7	Expenses		Input	−10	
8	Depreciation		Input	−4	
9	PBIT		Output	26	
10	GP%		Output	0.666667	
11					
12	Key:				
13	COS = cost of sales				
14	GP = gross profit = SUM (D4:D5)				
15	PBIT = profit before interest & taxation				
16	GP% = gross profit percentage = (D6/D4)				

Note the formulae (shown in the formula bar) for the output cells:

$$GP\ (D6) = SUM(D4:D5)$$
$$PBIT\ (D9) = SUM(D6:D8)$$
$$GP\%\ (D10) = (D6/D4)$$

The value of an input may be affected by variable factors over time; for example, the rate of inflation. This can be calculated on a spreadsheet as demonstrated below.

FIGURE 4.5 Sales and profit forecast with 3% p.a. inflation

	A	B	C	D	E
1	**Sales and profit forecast with 3% p.a. inflation**				
2			2013	2014	
3	Sales	Input	60	61.8	
4	COS (cost of sales)	Input	−20	−20.6	
5	GP (gross profit)	Output	40	41.2	

Note that base input data has been entered in C3 and C4.

$$\text{The output for C5} = \text{SUM(C3:C4)}$$
$$\text{D3} = (\text{C3}*1.03)$$
$$\text{D4} = (\text{C4}*1.03)$$
$$\text{D5} = \text{SUM(D3:D4)}$$

On this spreadsheet only enter new input data in the column 'C'. Always check on the formula bar that there is no embedded formula in a cell before you enter any new data.

Direct and derived input data

In the above simple examples you will have noted that we input direct data to arrive at outputs. Some of those outputs may then be used for input data (or input data that has been derived from other data or formulae).

Some variables are related to other variables within the input list. Variables derived from within the model are sometimes referred to as endogenous. Direct variables can be referred to as exogenous. This differentiation in the source of data is useful since the modeller will always be trying to reduce the amount of data that needs to be collected.

When using internal databases for input data you might consider the use of data mining processes. Data mining is the process of discovering patterns from large data sets by finding and extracting knowledge from a data set. This is carried out through the analysis of large quantities of data to extract previously unknown and informative patterns such as groupings of data records, anomalies and dependencies.

Important variables

Some variables are more important than others and will have a higher impact on the value of outputs. One way of determining this is to run a sensitivity analysis. This is done by removing one variable factor/input at a time and replacing it with another value. Then see what impact this has on the final result. This can be done when the model is run against various scenarios and we will discuss this in a later chapter.

The modeller will want to test for the relative importance of variables. However, it will sometimes be obvious that certain variables are not significant to the final outcome of output values. For example, it is not likely that the price of paint will have a major effect on a business case for an oil platform construction project even though paint is used.

Summary

Identify all of the inputs/variables that are needed to produce outputs. Use a simple input identification chart similar to the one shown in Figure 4.1. You will find a spreadsheet useful for this.

Prepare a database of inputs, identify how inputs relate to outputs and establish dependencies. Consider the use of data mining processes to discover patterns, anomalies and dependencies from large data sets.

Ensure the quality of data. For internal data use data extraction and cleansing tools if these are available.

Prepare a table of input data showing the unit of measure.

Prepare a schedule of formulae that are needed to apply to data in order to produce outputs. I use a spreadsheet for this similar to Figures 4.4 and 4.5.

Identify the relationships between variables and also determine how each one might influence the final output and result. Some variables will have a high impact whilst others may have little impact on the final result.

CHAPTER FIVE

SCENARIO IDENTIFICATION

Determining scenarios

We have discussed in the previous chapter that some variables will have a high impact of the final output and results derived from your business model. If the probability of a variation in the value of a high-impact item of input is high then the effect of changes in value of this type of input will also be high. When developing scenarios the modeller will have regard to high-impact items.

To determine different scenarios start with the high-impact items and then consider how various factors and events might affect them (see Figure 5.1).

The probability of an event occurring is shown in brackets. For example, there is a 60% chance of Corporation Tax being 35%.

From this list of possible events and their probability the modeller can talk with the decision team and other stakeholders and obtain their opinions as to the most likely path of events. For the purpose of this example we will assume that the shaded areas are the most likely path of events and the selected scenario. This can be the first scenario that is run. The assumptions used in this scenario will be listed and the scenario can be named.

Having run the first scenario it is then normal to run several other likely scenarios as identified by the decision makers and stakeholders. It is normal to select scenarios that are quite different in order to view the business from different perspectives. Scenarios that have a very low probability of actually happening are probably not worth running.

FIGURE 5.1 Scenario identification – possible events

Input (high level of impact on output result)	Possible event and probability 1	Possible event and probability 2	Possible event and probability 3	Possible event and probability 4
Sales price and volume (customer impact)	15% increase in demand (po.1) = increase in price and volume	10% increase in demand (po.15) = increase in price and volume	5% increase in demand (p.2) = increase in price and volume	5% reduction in demand (po.01) = reduction in price and volume
Sales price and volume (competitor impact)	15% increase in competitor prices (po.1) = increase in price and volume	10% increase in competitor prices (po.15) = increase in price and volume	5% increase in competitor prices (po.2) = increase in price and volume	5% reduction in competitor prices (po.01). New entrants (po.2) = reduction in price and volume
Material prices	15% increase raw material costs (po.1)	10% increase in raw material costs (po.15)	5% increase in raw material costs (po.2)	5% reduction in raw material costs (po.01)
Material usage	5% reduction in waste (po.1) = reduced material costs	2% reduction in waste (po.15) = reduced material costs	1% reduction in waste (po.2) = reduced material costs	5% increase in waste (po.1) = increased material costs
Labour rates	6% wage award (po.1)	4% wage award (po.2)	2% wage award (po.1)	No labour rate increase (po.001)
Labour efficiency	5% productivity increase (po.1)	3% productivity increase (po.15)	1% productivity increase (po.2)	2% loss in productivity (po.1)
Energy prices	10% rise due to Middle East tensions (po.2)	7% rise due to Middle East tensions (po.15)	5% rise due to Middle East tensions (po.1)	No increase due to alternative kick-in (po.01)
Interest rates	Base rate 0.5% (po.7)	Base rate 0.75% (po.5)	Base rate 1.5% (po.2)	Base rate2.% (po.1)
Exchange rate NZ$:£	2.1 (po.5)	1.99 (po.75)	1.90 (po.6)	1.85 (po.2)
Corporation Tax	35% (po.6)	30% (po.75)	28% (po.2)	25% (po.1)
Regulation	5% increase in H&S budget (po.9)	3% increase in H&S budget (po.7)	2% increase in H&S budget (po.5)	No increase in H&S budget (po.1)

Once the value of scenarios has been calculated it will then be possible to run a sensitivity analysis. This is done by removing one variable at a time and replacing it with another value in order to see how sensitive the final outcomes are to each variable. It will then be possible to focus on the important variables and finding ways to reduce risk and increase certainty.

Each scenario can also be run under a number of 'cases'. For example: Scenario 1 (high demand); Scenario 2 low interest rate.

It is always useful to have a process for developing scenarios. I have seen many different methods used but the above process is a useful guide.

You may also want to consider the following points when preparing your table. First of all consider the scope of the analysis and the intended users:

- Is it confined to an industry?
- Is it intended to cover a broader environment and range of issues?
- Is it intended to enable stakeholder participation?

Break down the process into a number of steps. There is no set method or best way to undertake each of the steps listed below but they will serve as a guide:

- Identify the users and stakeholders.
- Select participants.
- Define the scope of the scenarios.
- Identify the nature of the scenarios.
- Define units of measure, indicators, drivers and targets.
- Understand uncertainty and probability of events occurring.
- List scenarios and communicate these to stakeholders.
- Seek stakeholder input and refine all of the above points.
- Undertake analysis both qualitative and quantitative.

Some of the above steps may not be needed in a scenario process you are considering. Also, the amount of quantitative and qualitative analysis required will vary between one scenario process and another. You may use other scenario studies as a guide to start off your own process to save time, but be sure not to restrict your research by doing this. On the whole it is better to start afresh with a blank sheet and then compare your own scenarios with those of a previous/existing model just to see if you have omitted anything.

Populating the spreadsheet with input values and formulae

Having decided upon a scenario it is necessary to populate a spreadsheet with quantified input data. Every item of input must have a numerical value. The inputs will be linked to the final outputs by formulae, which will be added to the model spreadsheet.

Use the Financial Functions within Excel formula.

Example

What would be the monthly repayments on a loan of £300,000 for 15 years with an interest rate of 5% and monthly repayments?

1 Populate a spreadsheet with the base data of 300,000, 5%, 15 years, 12 ppa. See Figure 5.2 below.
2 Go to 'Formulas', 'Financial' and then drop-down menu to PMT to display an input form.
3 Under Rate insert B4/D4.
4 Under Nper insert C4*D4.
5 Under Pv insert A4.
6 Click OK.

The result is shown in cell E4 as £2,372.38

FIGURE 5.2 Adding formulae to the spreadsheet

	A	B	C	D	E	F
1	**Entering formulae**					
2			Duration	Payments	Monthly	
3	Cost	Int Rate	in years	p.a.	repayment	
4	300,000	5%	15	12	−2,372.38	
5						

Note that the PMT formula is: = PMT(B4/D4,C4*D4,A4)

Running different scenarios

Having input the data and formulae in Figure 5.2 above you might now want to experiment with different scenarios or different values.

For example, show on the spreadsheet what the monthly repayments would be for different durations of 20, 25 and 30 years.

Go back to the spreadsheet and drag down all the columns using the Fill handle. As you would expect, the monthly repayment reduces. This may ease monthly cash flow but, of course, will result in higher total repayments over the longer duration. Whether this is an attractive option will depend upon a number of factors, not least a company's cost of capital.

FIGURE 5.3 Running different scenarios

	A	B	C	D	E	F
1	**Running different scenarios**					
2			Duration	Payments	Monthly	
3	Cost	Int Rate	in years	p.a.	repayment	
4	300,000	5%	15	12	−2,372.38	
5	300,000	5%	20	12	−1,979.87	
6	300,000	5%	25	12	−1,753.77	
7	300,000	5%	30	12	−1,610.46	
8						

Having run different scenarios to loan periods you can also run scenarios for interest rates. You can see how this can also be used for running a sensitivity analysis by replacing one input value at a time with another and seeing the effect on the final result.

This table can represent a high or final level output or it can be input data and linked into another spreadsheet. For example, the monthly repayments might form a part of a bigger analysis.

Using Excel Scenario Manager for what-if analysis

Excel has a simple tool called 'Scenario Manager' that can be used for what-if analysis.

To use this:

1 Open a work sheet and enter your data. Refer to Figure 5.4.

2 Select the 'Data' tab.

3 Select 'What-If Analysis' under Data Tools.

4 Drop down and click on 'Scenario Manager'.

5 Click on Add and in the 'Add Scenario' box enter scenario name and then click on the worksheet cell that you want to change value. Unclick the prevent changes box. Then click 'OK'

6 This will bring up a 'Scenarios Value' box. Enter the interest rate you require. Click 'OK'.

7 The 'Scenario Manager' box will now show. Click 'Show' to see the new scenario data calculated in column B.

You can add a whole table of rates and quickly show re-calculated interest.

FIGURE 5.4 Excel's Scenario Manager for what-if analysis

	A	B	C	D	E	F
1	What-if analysis using Excel Scenario Manager					
2						
3	Principal	139,000				
4	Rate p.a.	10%				
5	Interest	13,900				
6						

You can enter a whole table of interest rates into Scenario Manager and then show the revised interest amount by selecting 'show' on the Scenario Manager table you have created. This can save time.

Scenarios versus projections

Projecting past figures and trends into the future is an easy way of predicting what might happen in the short term. However, in the medium to longer term it is not a lot of use doing this because no allowance has been made for fundamental changes in socio/economic, political or other qualitative changes. The effects of these changes can often be valued and this is where scenario planning provides real value. Scenario analysis and planning considers threads, linkages and combinations of variables and how the values of input data might be created and changed over time. For example, an earthquake in country 'A' may weaken its currency, making imports of raw materials from 'A' by country 'B' less expensive and thereby reducing country 'B''s cost of production. Feeding this sequence through a business model with a probability placed on earthquakes is an example of how scenario planning improves on simple trend projections. That is not to say that projections do not have their place, they do.

Scenario planning brings together known and unknown factors into a number of views of the future and the evaluation of these views can now be helped by the use of Excel.

Summary

In this chapter we have shown how to identify scenarios and introduced some simple methods that will give structure to your approach in what is a subjective topic. We have shown how to populate spreadsheets with basic data and formulae using Excel tool bars. We have used this data to run different scenarios. I have introduced you to Excel's Scenario Manager and how to build a Scenario Manager table when using an Excel sheet in order to save time.

Scenario-type analysis has many advantages over simple trend projections in that it considers many factors that might affect a variable's value and considers threads and linkages between variables and wider factors. You will need to be able to answer what-if questions and Scenario Manager can assist in this. I find it most useful to prepare a simple sensitivity table as in Figure 5.5 below to help managers focus on what is important.

FIGURE 5.5 Hypothetical effect of changes in variable on net profit

Variable	Movement in variable value	Percentage change in net profit
Interest rate	1% change in rate	−5.0
Material costs	5% cost increase	−1.0
Labour rates	5% rate increase	−2.0
General overheads	5% increase	−3.0
Sale prices	5% increase	+10
Sales volumes	5% increase	+10

Keep your team focused on what is important to the bottom line. Remember that a 10% increase in selling prices can be worth twice as much on the bottom line as a 10% reduction in costs!

	Budget	Actual	
Selling price	100	110	(+10%)
Cost	50	50	
Profit	50	60	(+20%)
Selling price	100	100	
Cost	50	45	(−10%)
Profit	50	55	(−10%)

Simple facts like this are easily forgotten in a heated, executive team debate. The purpose of business and financial modelling is to keep things on track and add clarity and focus on what is important rather than to provide lots of clever data so that the team cannot see the woods for the trees. Keep focused on what is important and avoid unnecessary complexity.

CHAPTER SIX

BUILDING A SIMPLE MODEL

Process

In this chapter we will build a simple business model using the following process:

FIGURE 6.1 Building and running a model

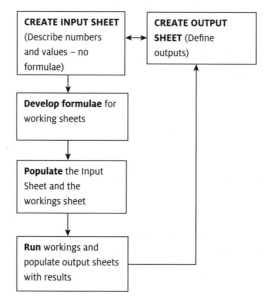

The basic instructions and things to remember that were discussed in previous chapters are:

1 Ensure the quality of your input data.
2 Check your assumptions are reasonable and make sense.
3 Ensure that formulae are correct by testing.
4 Ensure the model is dynamic and that output changes with any input change.
5 Test and validate each line of the model.

Example

Prepare a financial model that shows the profit after interest and taxation for a company that has the following base data:

Sales volume	100,000 units p.a.
Unit selling price	£5
Material cost per unit	£1
Labour cost per unit	£2
Overheads	£50,000
Cost of borrowing (interest)	8%
Term loan	£50,000

1 Prepare the output sheet for a business and financial model that shows the following:

Sales
Gross margin
Overheads
PBIT
Interest
Net profit after interest and before taxation

2 Prepare the input data sheets
3 Prepare the working sheets
4 Run the model for the above base case
5 Run the model for a case assuming 4% p.a. inflation on all costs and interest rates at 10% p.a.
6 How sensitive is the base case to a 1% increase in interest rates?

FIGURE 6.2 (1) Output sheet

	A	B	C	D	E	F	G	H
1	Output (sheet 1)							
2			Base case	Case 2	Sensitivity to 1% increase in interest			
3	Sales		£500,000	£500,000		£500,000		
4	COS		-£300,000	-£312,000		-£300,000		
5	GM		£200,000	£188,000		£200,000		
6	Overheads		-£50,000	-£52,000		-£50,000		
7	PBIT		£150,000	£136,000		£150,000		
8	Interest		-£4,000	-£5,000		-£4,500		
9	NP		£146,000	£131,000		£145,500		

Prepare the basic output sheet as above showing the headings required and a column for each case. Gross Margin, PBIT and Net Profit are derived from values in the column so show formulae as follows:

Gross Margin: = SUM(C3:C4) PBIT = SUM(C5:C6)
= SUM(D3:D4) = SUM(D5:D6)
= SUM(E3:E4) = SUM(E5:E6)

NP = SUM(C7:C9)
= SUM(D7:D9)
= SUM(E7:E9)

Populate the sheet with some small values in order to test the accuracy of the formulae.

FIGURE 6.2 (2) Input data sheet and workings

	A	B	C	D	E	F	G	H	I
1	Input data & working (sheet 2)								
2	INPUT DATA			Base case	4% infl	10% int	9% int		
3	Sales volume			100,000	100,000	100,000			
4	Unit selling price			£5	£5				
5	Material cost per unit			-£1	-£1.04				-£1.04
6	Labour cost per unit			-£2	-£2.08				
7	COS per unit			-£3	-£3.12				
8	Overheads			£50,000	£52,000	£52,000			
9	Interest rate			8%		10%	9%		
10	Loan			-£50,000		-£50,000	-£50,000		
11	4% inflation			1.04					
12	10% interest			0.1					
13	9% interest			0.09					
14									
15	WORKINGS								
16	Sales			£500,000	£500,000	£500,000			
17	COS			-£300,000	-£312,000				
18	Interest			-£4,000		-£5,000	-£4,500		

Input data

Populate sheet 2 column D with the input data.

Workings

Sales, Cost of Sales (COS) and Interest need to be derived from the workings. Enter formulae in column D as follows:

$$Sales = D3*D4$$
$$Unit\ COS = SUM(D5:D6)$$
$$COS = D3*D7$$
$$Interest = D9*D10$$

The values for sales, cost of sales and interest can now be entered onto the output sheet to give the final base case net profit after interest of £146,000.

To show the effect of 4% p.a. inflation and 10% interest p.a. add two more columns to the working sheet. Show an inflation column (base column × 1.04). Input the revised interest rate. Insert formulae to cells.

$$Material\ cost = D5*D11$$
$$Labour\ cost = D6*D11$$
$$COS\ per\ unit = SUM(E5:E6)$$
$$COS\ after\ infl. = E3*E7$$
$$Interest = F9*F10$$

The revised values for cost of sales after inflation of 4% and for interest at 10% are:

Cost of sales after 4% inflation	£312,000
Interest at 10%	£5,000

These values are now transferred to the output sheet to give a revised Net Profit of £131,000.

Sensitivity analysis

Add another column to the working sheet to show a 1% increase in interest (from 8% to 9%).

Revised interest after a 1% increase on the base case rate is £4,500: = G9*G10.

Therefore, a 1% increase in interest reduces profits by 0.3% (£500/£146,000).

Remember that the 1% increase in interest rates is an increase from 8% p.a. to 9% p.a. This is an effective increase of 1/8th. Figure 6.3 below shows that interest rates have little effect on profits:

FIGURE 6.3 Sensitivity of profits to interest rate increases

	A	B	C	D	E	F	G
1	Sensitivity of profits to increases in interest rates						
2							
3							
4	Int rate	9%	10%	11%			
5	Interest rate of increase	13%	25%	38%			
6	Profit change	−0.30%	−0.68%	−1.03%			
7							

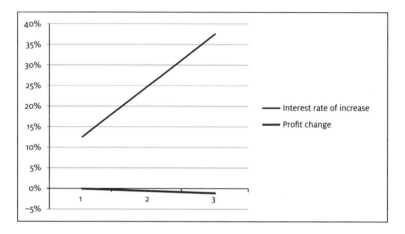

Answers:

Base case = Net Profit £146,000
Case 2, 4% inflation, 10% interest = Net Profit £131,000
Sensitivity to 1% increase in interest = 0.3% reduction in net profit

The results for this company show that its profits are not particularly sensitive to changes in interest rates. However, profits are sensitive to inflation. The graph shown in Figure 6.4 below shows how sensitive profits are to inflation. Note that I have used the graph facility in Microsoft's Excel 2007. If you are using Excel 2010 you might also use the convenient 'Sparkline' facility.

FIGURE 6.4 Sensitivity of profits to inflation

	A	B	C	D	E	F	G
1	**Sensitivity of profits to inflation**						
2	**Output**						
3	Inflation	0	4%	5%	6%	7%	
4	Profit % of base	100%	91%	79%	63%	44%	
5	PBIT	150,000	136,000	117,800	94,868	66,509	
6	**Input**						
7	Sales	500,000	500,000	500,000	500,000	500,000	
8	All costs	−350,000	−364,000	−382,200	−405,132	−433,491	
9	PBIT	150,000	136,000	117,800	94,868	66,509	
10	Infl 4%	1.04					
11	Infl 5%	1.05					
12	Infl 6%	1.06					
13	Infl 7%	1.07					

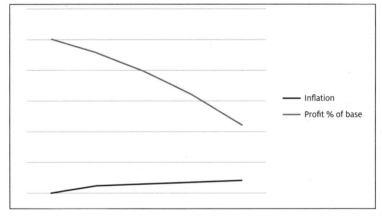

For this sensitivity analysis first of all define the outputs on the spreadsheet. In this case they are:

> Profits before interest and Taxation (PBIT) before inflation (base profits)
> Profits after inflation
> Profits after inflation expressed as a percentage of base profits

Head up the sheet's columns for 0%, 4%, 5%, 6% and 7% inflation rates.

The effect of inflation on profits can then be compared to the percentage changes in base profits by using the required data and formula.

Next define the input required and populate the spreadsheet with the input required. This is:

Sales	500,000	
All costs	350,000	
PBIT	Sales less	All Costs = SUM(B7:B8)
Inflation 4%	1.04	
Inflation 5%	1.05	
Inflation 6%	1.06	
Inflation 7%	1.07	

Now complete the formula for each output cell:

Starting with the 4% inflation column:

All costs	= B8*B10
PBIT	= SUM(C7:C8)
Profit % of base	= C5/B5

Complete formulae for the 5%, 6% and 7% columns. Of course, using Excel you do not need to type these in. For example enter = in the working cell, select the first input cell required, enter the operator category required (addition, subtraction, multiplication, division) and then the next input cell required. This will compute the value. To see the actual embedded formula on any cell simply click on the cell and the formulae will be seen in the formula bar above the sheet.

To prepare a graph:

Select the rows 3 and 4
Open the insert tab
Select line graph

If the type of graph is not to your liking select another style or re-format.

The graph shows at a glance how fast profits dive with every 1% increase in inflation. By undertaking a sensitivity analysis for each variable and item of input it is possible to see immediately the effect of any changes.

When undertaking a sensitivity analysis only replace one variable at a time in order to see what the effect of a change in that variable's value will have on profits.

This example has been kept simple in order to demonstrate the basics of model building, scenario planning and sensitivity analysis. We have not used the full potential of Excel so that we don't camouflage the basic principals of model building.

Data extraction using Excel pivot tables

You might only require some of the data from an input sheet to prepare a report. To do this you can extract data manually or, to save time and ensure accuracy, you might want to use a data extraction tool. If your data is on Excel then you can use the pivot table tool for extraction. An example of this is given in Figure 6.5.

FIGURE 6.5 Using Excel pivot tables for data extraction

	A	B	C	D	E	F
1	Using Excel pivot tables for data extraction					
2	Input data					
3	Month	Product	Vol	Price £		
4	1	B	200	3		
5	2	A	300	2		
6	3	B	100	3		
7	4	B	300	3		
8	5	A	300	2		
9	6	A	100	2		
10			1300			
11					Pivot table analysis by product	
12					Row Labels	Sum of Vol
13					A	700
14					B	600
15					Grand Total	1300
16						

To follow this example:

1 Enter your input data onto a worksheet. In this example we have shown product sales, volumes and prices by month for a six-month period.

2 We now want to find out what the total sales were for each product during the period. You can imagine how difficult this would be for

a large volume of data spanning several years and multiple products. I have kept this example very simple to demonstrate how to use the pivot tool.

3 Highlight/select the data table.

4 Insert tab.

5 Pivot table and drop down to pivot table.

6 A create pivot table box will show on your sheet.

7 I have selected the table range from the input table and chosen a location to show the new table on the existing worksheet. You can choose other options.

8 Another box will appear titled 'Pivot Table Field List'.

9 I ticked the boxes for product and volume.

10 The pivot table then shows on the sheet in the location you selected.

You can now see the total volumes for products A and B.

It is worthwhile experimenting with the pivot table tool to become proficient.

Some reminders of best practice

- Don't get carried away with the fun and ease of Excel modelling and end up solving the wrong problem really well.

- Make sure you are setting the correct question – the visual thinking techniques described in earlier chapters should help you to do this.

- Use whatever tools you like depending upon the resources available in your organization. For example, some build applications with an Excel front-end and a SQL Server DB back-end.

- If using Excel take care if you are linking sheets within a workbook. Take even more care if you are linking workbooks. Errors can cascade throughout the whole model.

- Of course, you will back up all data continually! For example make sure files are also stored on a network drive and not just your own laptop. You may also back up on a memory stick or external hard drive.

- Save the model regularly either at the completion of a critical stage or, like me, every five minutes when I remember!

- Keep things as simple as possible. For example, when using Excel avoid hiding columns or rows if at all possible. A model builder might easily forget that there is hidden data and type over it thereby ruining the model.
- Remember that a person with expert modelling skills in a tool such as Excel might not be the best person when it comes to understanding the business and asking the right questions. Avoid ownership falling into the hands of someone who, whilst being technically excellent, leads you into solving the wrong problem.
- Business modelling is more than just projecting the past into a future predicted environment. It needs to consider and evaluate new business opportunities.
- A simple and robust Excel model is often better than one that uses all the features available but is vulnerable to mistakes and misuse.

Reasons for failure of a model and how to avoid them

Sometimes business and financial models that have taken months to prepare are not used or simply fail to provide any information that is of use to an executive team. Here are some of the common reasons for failure.

Lack of executive sponsorship

A model that is not sponsored and supported with some enthusiasm by the decision-making team in an organization just won't get started. If there is no ownership or understanding of how the model works and what it can produce then it is unlikely that it will be seriously used and updated. It will just become redundant.

Users who don't understand

Time needs to be taken to train users in using the model. A guide as to how to actually use the model is essential. As a developer you will be close to the model and all of its quirks! A user will not and, as a consequence, will quickly get bored trying to understand the model and cease to use it.

Lack of confidence amongst stakeholders

A model will have many stakeholders and they need to be confident that their requirements are met in a reliable way. They need confidence in the quality of the input and in the mechanics of the model. Auditors, for example, will want to be sure that the outcome of any calculations, such as depreciation, are correct and auditable. A model that has been over-engineered is unnecessarily complex and has an illogical process flow will not inspire confidence. Keeping Excel financial models as simple as possible will increase stakeholder confidence. External data inputs need to be recognized as such and referenced.

Errors

Errors in any cell value will ruin confidence. The model has to be 100% accurate. Data input and cell formula checks and tests need to be undertaken on internal and imported data. The quality of a model will be measured by its weakest link.

Lack of understanding by key users

The model developer and custodian needs to be backed up just as all data is backed up. It is no use relying on one person who might leave, become ill or go to the happy hunting ground. At least two people need to fully understand the model.

Changes in source cells not being reflected in updated formula

When a source cell changes formula needs to be changed. Pivot tables do not automatically update to reflect changes in source data. If a model relies on pivot tables these will need updating. There are many dangers in cell changes not being reflected in formula.

Model capacity for change

A model needs to be able to cope with future changes. For example, it needs built-in capacity to be able to accept additional assets or business activities.

The basics

Business and financial models need to be kept as simple and robust as possible. An elegant and clever model might not necessarily be as robust as a simple one. Design for longevity, flexibility, user clarity and a clear audit trail.

Summary

In this chapter we have shown a process for building a simple business model using the basics of Excel spreadsheets:

- Define the outputs first.
- Set up a column on the output sheet for each case.
- Only use formulae for column totals.
- Set up an input sheet for all basic data.
- Set up working formulae that are to be applied to the input data to produce outputs.
- Transfer output values to output sheet.
- Run sensitivity analysis as required for each case.
- Use pivot tables to extract data and summarize different fields.

You will notice that I did not link sheets! I have seen time and again problems that linking sheets can create. It can be a recipe for disaster when things eventually go wrong, which they inevitably do! It is a way of building imbedded errors where the data in one sheet can be destroyed by changing data in another. When things go wrong it can take a lot of effort to unpick. The whole model can become very fragile. Placing data into a formulae cell will cascade an error throughout the whole model. However, linking sheets can save time if done with care and there is an argument that the less manual input of data the less chance there is for error. Perhaps this is a case for individual judgement, which will depend upon your skill level in using Excel. Certainly linking sheets within a workbook is normal practice.

CHAPTER SEVEN

USING CHARTS

Excel charts

In the previous chapter we have used several charts to provide a quick picture of model results. I have used line charts since these quickly convey a message that may be hidden in the numbers. There are many types of chart available in Excel and I have given a few examples below in Figures 7.1 to 7.4.

A chart can be particularly useful when looking at turning points, payback periods or in break-even analysis.

Example

Consider the following profile:

A company's results in 2013 are:

Sales	$500,000
Costs	$400,000
Profit	$100,000
Profit as % of Sales	20%

Over the following eight years it is expected that sales values (price and volume) will increase by 5% p.a.

During the same period it is expected that costs will increase by 10% p.a.

How long will it be before the company starts to make a loss? Show the position graphically.

Solution

- Enter the data directly into an output sheet as shown in Figure 7.1.
- Highlight rows 2 and 3.
- Open the 'Insert' tab close to the top of the sheet.
- Go to Charts/Line and using the drop down choose a 2-D line chart.
- Your chart will now show on the sheet. Drag it to a convenient position on the sheet so that it does not hide your input data.
- Click onto the chart and open the 'Layout' tab at the top of the sheet.
- Under 'Labels' choose 'Axis Titles'.
- Using the drop down select 'Primary Horizontal Axis Title' and choose 'Title Below Axis'.
- You can now enter your horizontal axis title on the chart.
- Once again click on the chart and open the 'Layout' tab at the top of the sheet.
- Under 'Labels' choose 'Axis Titles'.
- Using the drop down select 'Primary Vertical Axis Title' and choose 'Horizontal Title'.
- Now enter your vertical axis title on the chart (in a horizontal form).

Your chart should now be displayed as in Figure 7.1.

FIGURE 7.1 Line chart

	A	B	C	D	E	F	G	H	I	J	K
1	Line chart										
2	Year	1	2	3	4	5	6	7	8	9	
3	Sales	500	525	551	579	608	638	670	704	739	
4	Costs	400	440	484	532	586	644	709	779	857	
5											

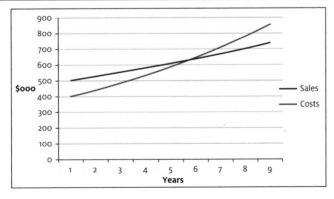

You will see on the graph that at a point during Year 5½ costs start to exceed the sales value. This means that it will only take the company about five years before it starts making a loss.

If costs increase by 10% when sales are only increasing at 5% then the company (which was making a 20% profit) will be making losses in only five years.

This graphical presentation demonstrates this point quickly and clearly.

Excel has a great selection of charts. Two others that might be used are shown in Figures 7.2 and 7.3.

FIGURE 7.2 Block chart

	A	B	C	D	E	F	G	H	I	J	K
1	Block chart or histogram										
2	Year	1	2	3	4	5	6	7	8	9	
3	Sales	500	525	551	579	608	638	670	704	739	
4	Costs	400	440	484	532	586	644	709	779	857	
5											

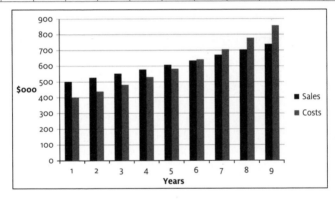

FIGURE 7.3 Three-dimensional line chart

	A	B	C	D	E	F	G	H	I	J	K
1	3-Dimensional line chart										
2	Year	1	2	3	4	5	6	7	8	9	
3	Sales	500	525	551	579	608	638	670	704	739	
4	Costs	400	440	484	532	586	644	709	779	857	
5											

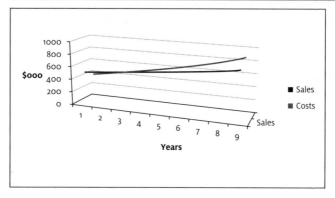

Using charts to help concentrate on the most important variables in an organization

Sometimes an executive team concentrate their attention on the wrong thing, or the least important thing. A simple bar chart showing how a 10% variance in each item affects the bottom line can help the team concentrate on the most important things first. Consider the following:

Sales $20K
Costs $10K
Profit $10K

Now, a 10% reduction in sales value is more serious than a 10% increase in costs. If sales reduce by 10% the effect will be a 20% reduction on the bottom line. However, if costs go up by 10% the effect on the bottom line in this case will be 10%. Therefore, an adverse sales variance is much worse than an adverse material price variance. This may seem obvious but it is often overlooked.

When considering all of the variables in an organization it is useful to prepare a chart that shows the relative effect that a variance in the value of each variable has on final profits. The following case will show how Excel can be used to demonstrate this using a bar chart.

Example

A company has the following budget:

Unit sales price $10
Sales volume   10,000 units
Unit material cost $5
Material usage   10,000 units

What has the greatest effect on bottom line profits, selling prices, sales volumes, material prices or materials used?

Solution

Enter the above data onto an Excel sheet as shown in Figure 7.4.

FIGURE 7.4 Table and chart showing importance of variables

	A	B	C	D	E	F	G	H
1	Importance of variables							
2	Variable		Affect of 10% variance on profits					
3	Selling prices		22%					
4	Sales volumes		20%					
5	Material prices		18%					
6	Material usage		10%					
7	Total variance		70%					
8			Budget	Actual	Variance	Price	Volume	% change
9	Sales price		10	11				10
10	Sales volume		10,000	11,000				10
11	Sales value		100,000	121,000	21,000	11,000	10,000	
12	% change				21%	11%	10%	
13	Material price		−5	−4				10
14	Material qty used		10,000	9,000				10
15	Material cost		−50,000	−36,000	14,000	9,000	5,000	
16	% change				28%	18%	10%	
17	Profits		50,000	85,000	35,000	20,000	15,000	

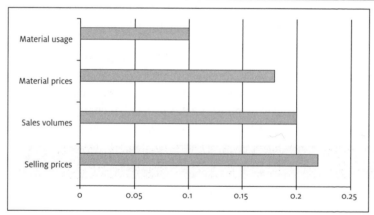

- Enter the budget data.
- Enter actual data – assume that all actuals are 10% favourable.
  For example, actual selling prices are budget plus 10%.
- Use the formula facility to calculate sales value, material cost and profit.
- Use the formula facility to calculate the total variances.

- Use the formula facility to calculate the variance analysis. For example:

  - Sales price = D10*(D9−C9)
  - Sales volume = C9*(D10−C10)
  - Material price = D14*(D13−C13)
  - Material usage = C13*(D14−C14)

- Calculate the percentage of each variance in relation to the budgeted profit. For example, the sale price variance is 22% of the budgeted profit:

  - Effect of 10% sales price variance on profit = F11/C17

- Highlight the area:

  - A   B   C
  - 3   22%
  - 4   20%
  - 5   18%
  - 6   10%

- Select 'Insert' – 'Charts' – 'Bar'

The chart clearly demonstrates that, in the case of this company, a 10% change in selling prices has a greater effect on profits than does a 10% change in material usage. You can do this for every variable in the organization to display a chart that helps management focus on items that are most important.

Charts for break-even analysis

Excel can be used for break-even-type charts. Key to this is constructing the input data and the output table in the correct form.

Example

A company produces bags at a cost of $4 per bag. It sells them for $11.50 per bag. It has fixed costs (overheads) of $4,000 p.a. How many bags should it sell to break even (that is to make no profit or loss).

The answer can be obtained by dividing the fixed costs ($4,000) by the unit contribution ($7.5 being $11.50 less $4). This will give a volume of 533. At this volume the fixed costs will be covered but there will be no profit.

Proof

```
533 units @ selling price $11.50    = $6,130 (sales value)
533 units @ unit variable cost $4 = $2,132 (variable costs)
Total contribution                  = $3,998
Fixed costs                         = $4,000
Profit                              = $2 (say zero)
```

This is easy enough to calculate manually. However, what if you want to try out different prices and costs and see what effect these had or see how much profit would be achieved at different volume levels? It is most useful to use Excel for this and Figure 7.5 shows how this can be done. It is easy to set up the table incorrectly and I have, therefore, shown this as an online template for you to use.

FIGURE 7.5 Break-even chart

	A	B	C	D	E	F	G
1	**Break-even chart**						
2	Inputs – assumptions						
3	Fixed cost assumption	$4,000					
4	Variable cost assumption	$4.00					
5	Number of units	50.00					
6	Unit price	$11.50					
7							
8		**Units**	**Revenue**	**Fixed Costs**	**Variable Costs**	**Total Costs**	**Total Profit**
9		0.00	$0	$4,000	$0	$4,000	$(4,000)
10		50.00	$575	$4,000	$200	$4,200	$(3,625)
11		100.00	$1,150	$4,000	$400	$4,400	$(3,250)
12		150.00	$1,725	$4,000	$600	$4,600	$(2,875)
13		200.00	$2,300	$4,000	$800	$4,800	$(2,500)
14		250.00	$2,875	$4,000	$1,000	$5,000	$(2,125)
15		300.00	$3,450	$4,000	$1,200	$5,200	$(1,750)
16		350.00	$4,025	$4,000	$1,400	$5,400	$(1,375)
17		400.00	$4,600	$4,000	$1,600	$5,600	$(1,000)
18		450.00	$5,175	$4,000	$1,800	$5,800	$(625)
19		500.00	$5,750	$4,000	$2,000	$6,000	$(250)
20		550.00	$6,325	$4,000	$2,200	$6,200	$125
21		600.00	$6,900	$4,000	$2,400	$6,400	$500
22		650.00	$7,475	$4,000	$2,600	$6,600	$875
23		700.00	$8,050	$4,000	$2,800	$6,800	$1,250
24		750.00	$8,625	$4,000	$3,000	$7,000	$1,625
25		800.00	$9,200	$4,000	$3,200	$7,200	$2,000
26							

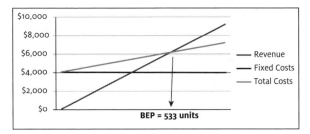

To construct the chart:

● Populate the sheet with the input data (assumptions).
● Head up an output table: Units/Revenue/Fixed Costs/Variable Costs/ Total Costs/Total Profit.
● Insert formula to each cell. For example:
  – C10 – Revenue   = B10*B6
  – D10 – Fixed costs   = B3
  – E10 – Variable costs   = B10*B4
  – F10 – Total costs   = E10+D10
  – G10 – Total profit   = C10–F10

Continue this method for all cells. Of course, with Excel you do not have to actually type in the formula – just click on the cell you want to use in the formula. There are many good books on using Excel and you can learn by just practising using and trying out the various functions and help guides in the tool. Alternatively you can go on a short Excel user course. These usually last two days. There are also various Excel user groups on social networking sites such as 'LinkedIn'. For those who are more advanced in Excel use I have included a list of shortcuts in the Appendix. However, you do not need to use them for the purpose of this book. Remember that keeping things simple makes more robust models.

- Highlight the output table.
- INSERT/CHARTS/LINE/2-D Line.
- Drag the chart to a convenient place on your spreadsheet.

Chart tools

You may need to change the layout of your chart. For example, you might want to switch rows and columns. To do this click on the chart and a CHART TOOLS tab will show at the top of the sheet towards the right. Click on this and you will find a number of options to change your chart. To switch rows and columns click on 'Switch Row/Column' and this will be reflected for you on your chart.

Presenting data and charts to communicate clearly

Data presented in an ad-hoc manner will not convey your message clearly. If you import a table that is in a confused form you can re-format it using Excel's formatting tools. For example, you might have a table of sales of products and want to re-format the table to show the sales in order of size/importance. You may also want your graph to show sales in this way. Figure 7.6 shows how this is done in Excel by using the formatting tool.

FIGURE 7.6 Presenting graphs to communicate clearly

	A	B	C	D	E	F	G	H
1	**Presenting graphs to communicate clearly**							
2	**Sales**							
3		2013	2014	2015	2016	2017		
4	Pumps	300	330	340	350	370		
5	Filter	100	120	140	200	260		
6	Hoses	50	55	60	65	70		
7	Pipes	75	80	85	90	95		
8	Taps	90	95	100	110	115		
9	Tanks	600	650	660	670	690		
10	**Sales – sorted by significance**							
11		2013	2014	2015	2016	2017		
12	Hoses	50	55	60	65	70		
13	Pipes	75	80	85	90	95		
14	Taps	90	95	100	110	115		
15	Filter	100	120	140	200	260		
16	Pumps	300	330	340	350	370		
17	Tanks	600	650	660	670	690		
18								

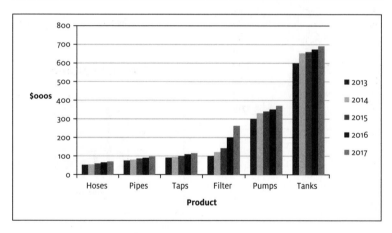

Highlight the jumbled data in the first table, right click, sort and then choose how you want to sort – smallest to largest, etc. This will then sort your data as is shown in the second table. Highlight the second table – insert – graph – bar chart and you will have your chart in an order that is more meaningful to users.

Using Excel pivot charts to show extracted data

In the previous chapter I described the Excel pivot tool. There is also a pivot chart tool that can show extracted data in a chart form. An example of this is given in Figure 7.7.

FIGURE 7.7 Using Excel pivot tables and charts

	A	B	C	D	E	F	G
1	Using Excel pivot tables and charts						
2	Input data						
3	Month	Product	Vol	Price		Row Labels	Sum of Vol
4	1	B	200	3		A	700
5	2	A	300	2		B	680
6	3	B	100	3		C	150
7	4	B	300	3		D	110
8	5	A	300	2		E	120
9	6	A	100	2		F	150
10	7	B	80	3		Grand Total	1910
11	8	C	90	4			
12	9	E	120	6			
13	10	D	110	5			
14	11	C	60	4			
15	12	F	150	8			
16			1910				
17							
18							
19							
20							
21							
22							
23							
24							

Product volumes chart (F11:G23 area):

Product volumes — bar chart, Volumes axis 0 to 800, Products A B C D E F, series Total.

Instructions for use:

1 Insert your input data onto the sheet.

2 Decide which columns and rows you want to extract data from and show on a chart. In this case we want to show the volumes for each product.

3 Open the Insert tab and click on the drop down menu of the Pivot Table.

4 Select pivot chart and highlight the columns/rows you have chosen to extract data from.

5 A 'Create pivot table' should now show on your worksheet.

6 Select a table or range. This should show the columns and rows you have already selected from your data table.

7 Choose where you want the Pivot Table/Chart to be placed. In this case it is the existing worksheet.

8 Select the columns and rows on the sheet where you want the Pivot Table/Chart to be placed.

9 Click into the location box.

10 Click OK.

11 Under the now showing Pivot Table Field list choose product and volume.

12 Your pivot chart with table will now appear.

This can be a very useful tool to quickly extract data and show on a chart. Using Excel functions and tools is a bit like riding a bike and to become proficient it is best to get stuck in and start using it. Some readers will already be proficient and for those I have included a list of shortcuts in the Appendix that might prove useful.

Summary

In this chapter we have described some Excel charts that will be useful in modelling. Charts can be used when explaining an important point to an executive team. Excel is a valuable charting tool. Ensure that you construct the data table correctly so that the chart shows the picture in the way you want it to. You will need to use the Excel chart tool regularly to become proficient at charting. Sometimes you will need to extract certain cells in a spreadsheet for charting and the Excel pivot chart tool will do this for you and ensure accuracy.

CHAPTER EIGHT

MODELLING BUDGETS

In this chapter we will describe budget relationships that can be incorporated into financial models.

Planning and budgeting

Budgets are prepared from and aligned to company plans and monitor performance. A budget should be the financial evaluation of a plan. Accordingly the budget process follows on from an initial business plan. It is also part of a planning process because once the financial consequences of a plan of action are known the plan may need to be revised. A typical planning and budgeting process is shown in Figure 8.1.

The planning and budgeting process shown in Figure 8.1 demonstrates how budgeting needs to be integrated with the planning process. As far as possible budgets should be zero-based. Zero-based budgets (ZBB) assume that each year the budget holder starts from scratch and has to justify each item of expenditure to support the operational strategy, key tasks and goals. Some budgets will be dependent upon other budgets. For example, a production budget may be dependent upon a sales budget. A budget for new plant and equipment (a capital budget) might be dependent upon the requirements of production. Each business will have its own budgeting hierarchy and budget dependencies. Knowing these dependencies needs to be understood before a financial model using Excel can be prepared.

FIGURE 8.1 A planning and budgeting process

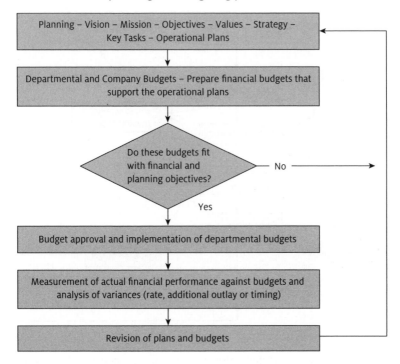

Typical planning and budgeting dependencies that can be modelled using Excel are shown in Figure 8.2.

This illustration shows how certain budgets depend upon the completion of other budgets and that all budgets must support the overall organizational goals and operational strategy. The marketing plan and strategy will help kick off the sales budget, which in turn will form a basis for a production budget and a debtors' budget. The production budget will help budget for creditors, stocks and also identify plant and equipment (capital budget). This will form the budget for depreciation and also help identify any long-term funding. Departmental overhead budgets to support sales and production will be completed and budgets that affect cash flow will feed into the cash budget. Budgets affecting the profit and loss and balance sheet budgets will help the accountant complete a forecast financial position and this will then be fed back into the high-level planning process to see if the evaluated plans (budgets) are feasible. Plans and budgets are continually adjusted by budget holders

FIGURE 8.2 Budget dependencies

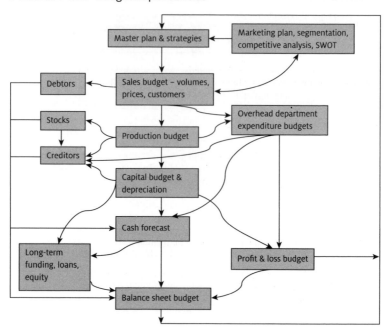

and executive teams as new information comes to light and this is why a budgeting process will usually takes some months to complete.

Much of what we have discussed so far will not be the responsibility of the financial modeller but will be undertaken by the accountant or financial director. However, having an understanding of the whole process will enable you to see how company budgets can be modelled and linked together. Linking budgets together using Excel provides a valuable tool for modelling and answering 'what if'-type questions.

Departmental budgets and variance analysis

Departmental budgets for operating costs and for capital equipment can conveniently be modelled using Excel. Operating costs are items such as salaries, rent, power, stationery, advertising, travel, accommodation, etc, whilst capital equipment costs are for fixed assets such as plant, equipment, vehicles, furniture, etc.

The first stage in a departmental budget is to estimate what resources your department needs to achieve the goals and key tasks that have been agreed as part of the overall planning process. In doing this you might want to consider what was spent in the previous year in order to get a feel for the cost of certain items. However, you should most definitely not simply take last year's actual costs and repeat them as the current year budget because this would not reflect zero-based budgeting! An allowance must also be made for inflation.

A departmental worksheet for the finance department's operating budget could look like this:

TABLE 8.1

Resource	2013 £000s	2014 £000s	Key task Reference	Comments
Salaries	210	218	3	Inflationary pay increase 4%
National insurance	11	12	3	Budget increase
Training	20	5	2	Reduction due to staff retention
Stationery	5	3	3	New supplier
Travel	20	5	4	Branch closure requires fewer trips
Recruitment costs	30	5	3	Expected staff retention
Entertainment	2	0	3	Not required
Accounting software	0	8	3	New software required at current prices
Share of overheads	16	17	3	Inflation increase 4%
Total	**314**	**273**		

Note that each item in the budget is related to a key task. Key tasks flow from the operational strategy and are usually given numbers. For example, key task number 3 could be 'to meet company statutory and legal obligations'. Some companies may not use the term key task but might use some other term. The point here is to remember that you will need to justify your expenditure and link it back to the overall organizational plan.

The 2013 column is for the previous year and is used as a guide only to see if costs are reasonable for undertaking a similar key task. They can also be helpful to ensure that items are not omitted.

An Excel spreadsheet can be used to feed your figures into the overall consolidated company budgets showing overall salaries, stationery costs, etc. It can also consolidate the costs of undertaking key tasks. For example, the cost of achieving key task 3 (meet company statutory and legal obligations) is £263K. The question can now be asked whether this task could be outsourced to a professional firm at a lower cost.

Some departments will require additional capital equipment. This is prepared on a different form from operating expenditure. A capital budget relates to the purchase of new fixed assets. Capital costs for fixed assets are not consumed within the budget year but may span many years. For example, a car might be used in the business for five years. Typical items of capital expenditure are plant and equipment, vehicles, furniture and fittings, buildings, improvement (not repairs) to existing assets and large mainframe-type computer installations. Smaller computers are often assumed to be written off in the year of purchase and are treated as operating expenditure rather then capital.

Capital budgets will have to be justified in that they must support the overall organizational goals. It may be that new plant is required for a new opportunity that has been identified in the plan or that there is an opportunity to improve efficiency. The planning process should recognize an opportunity, which will then be considered by the appropriate operating department. This will then be evaluated and a decision made as to whether to proceed or not. Capital expenditure will also have specific funding implications and additional long-term funds will need to be found.

Capital budget process:

- recognition of an opportunity;
- link with overall corporate goals;
- initial costings;
- identification of financial benefits;
- evaluation, net present value, payback, etc;
- identification of alternatives;
- proposal;
- decision.

Once the decision has been made to undertake the capital project the department responsible should submit details to the finance department. For example:

TABLE 8.2

Description of asset	Expected life in years	Cost £ooos	Month
Machine	5	50	June
Delivery van	6	30	September

The above input into the financial model will feed into the depreciation budget, the funding requirement and tax allowance calculations.

Reporting of actual expenditure against budget

Example of a year to date budget v actual expenditure report in £ooos:

TABLE 8.3

Resources	YTD budget	YTD actual	Total variance	Additional Rate	Additional Outlay	Additional Timing
Salaries	250	240	10			10
Travel	30	35	(5)	(5)		
Entertainment	10	5	5			5
Stationery	20	25	(5)			(5)
Training	30	40	(10)	(5)		(5)
Allocated overheads	70	70	0			
Totals	**410**	**415**	**(5)**	**(10)**	**0**	**5**

Notes:

1 Year to date (YTD) figures are shown only. This is generally the most informative level at which to report. A separate report can be prepared to show current month values if required.

2 A report similar to this will be prepared for each department.

3 The total variance is reported with adverse variances shown in brackets.

4 The analysis of the total variance can be explained in three columns: rate, additional outlay and timing. These should be completed by the budget holder.

5 Rate = a change in the rate (price) from that anticipated in the budget. For example, the budget may have assumed a 3% increase in training fees when in fact they increased by 10%.

6 Additional outlay = purchasing more (or less if favourable) of a resource but at the same price.

7 Timing = The expenditure is earlier or later than expected.

Example

Budget is for 10 rolls of paper @ £5 per roll	£50
Actual is 12 rolls of paper @ £4 per roll	£48
Total Variance is	£2 Favourable

Due to:

Additional Outlay – 2 rolls @ £5	£10 Adverse
Rate – 12 rolls @ (£4–£5)	£12 Favourable
Total Variance is	£2 Favourable

Most variances can be explained in the above categories of rate, additional outlay and timing. It is helpful if budget holders can use this discipline so that a consolidated variance analysis can be prepared. Budget holders will normally provide comments for the variances in addition to the analysis classifications.

Some key departmental budgets

Most organizations will require the managers of each department (the budget holders) to produce a budget. Budget holders should be responsible for the expenditure that they can control. Once their budget has been approved they will be responsible for controlling expenditure against their budget and this will be done at the point of commitment assisted by periodic reporting of actual against budgeted expenditure.

Key budgets in most organizations are:

Sales revenue budget

Production budget

Materials budget

Labour budget

Overhead budgets

Capital budget

Sales budget

The sales budget is one of the key budgets in an organization because most other departmental budgets depend upon and support the requirements of the sales budget. For example, the production and transportation budget will depend upon how much product is to be sold and delivered.

The sales budget will show volumes and prices for each product to be sold. The volume forecast to be sold will depend upon demand and the ability to compete and fulfil and the price will depend upon competitive factors, supply and demand.

When preparing a sales budget the sales director will take account of the following factors:

- the value of organizational growth required;
- the ability of the organization to manufacture and deliver;
- production capacity ceilings;
- demand for products and services;
- pricing;
- market trends and future direction;
- competition both existing and potential;
- organizational limiting factors;
- channels to market;
- distribution and operational strategies;

- marketing strategies;
- sales force ability and resources;
- advertising budget.

The price of a product is set by the market. In an efficient market it will be set by the interaction of supply and demand. Supply will be affected by competitors offering the same or alternative products. Demand will be affected by both the need for and the ability to purchase a product in a market. The sales director will work closely with the marketing director to determine both price and volume budgets. Setting a sales budget requires an in-depth understanding of the market and competition.

Excel can be used for plotting a line graph to show price elasticity. Use the vertical axis for prices and the horizontal axis for demand volumes. You would normally expect that demand volume will decrease when prices go up resulting in an inverse curve on your graph.

An example of a sales budget for a company selling rigid inflatable boats is given below:

TABLE 8.4

Product/model	Forecast volumes	Unit price £	Sales revenue £
3 metre	500	800	400,000
4 metre	300	1,000	300,000
5 metre	100	2,000	200,000
6 metre	50	5,000	250,000
Total			1,150,000

Before a sales budget is finally agreed a reality check is essential since there is no room for reckless optimism. This is because so many other things 'hang off' the sales budget. Production capacity, sales force recruitment, advertising budgets and capital budgets are just a few of the commitments that might depend on sales budget accuracy. A company could get into serious difficulty by getting the sales budget wrong. For example, one sales manager was optimistic that sales indications from an overseas agent were realistic! They were but they would end up in an existing fulfilled territory resulting in no additional sales.

A few final reality checks might include:

- What is the basis for the volume assumptions?
- What research has been undertaken to support the sales budget?
- Is there production capacity to meet the forecast sales volumes?
- Do forecast sales fit with the company's overall plans?
- Is the demand real?
- Are new increased volumes in new or existing territories?
- Are growth figures real?
- Are territory/volume assumptions correct?
- Have we correctly analysed the competition?
- Are prices realistic?
- How sensitive are prices to changes in demand?
- Can the marketing department really provide the promotion required?
- How accurate has the sales director been in the past with sales forecast?

When the sales budget has been agreed a company can proceed to prepare a production budget.

Production volume budget

The production volume budget will determine the production hours required to produce the volumes of products required in the sales budget taking into account any opening and closing stocks.

TABLE 8.5

Product/ model	Forecast sales volumes	Opening stock	Closing stock	Production required
3 metre	500	0	10	510
4 metre	300	20	20	300
5 metre	100	5	15	110
6 metre	50	2	12	60
Total production required				980

To meet the sales budget and the required stock level will require the building of 980 units. We now calculate production hours and also consider what affect this will have on plant capacity. To do this we will prepare a plant utilization budget.

TABLE 8.6

Product/ model	Production volume	Assembly unit hours	Assembly hours
3 metre	510	8	4,080
4 metre	300	10	3,000
5 metre	110	12	1,320
6 metre	60	12	720
Total assembly hours			9,120
Assembly plant capacity			9,000
Capacity shortage			(120)

We have identified a limiting factor. The assembly plant has a capacity shortage of 120 hours. A decision will now be made. Either increase plant capacity (this will have an effect on the capital budget and on the cash budget) or simply do not fulfil the sale budget volumes. This is an example of the iterative process that is part of budgeting and also an example of how the sales budget affects other budgets.

There will, of course, be many stages in the production of this product. We have just considered the assembly department. Other departments might include mouldings, painting and testing, each of which will have their own limiting factors.

Now that we have worked out the number of hours required in the assembly department we can prepare a direct labour budget and a direct materials budget.

Direct labour budget

The direct labour budget takes the required labour hours from the production budget and calculates the cost of labour using standard and overtime labour rates and the number of employees required.

Direct labour budget for assembly 2013

The assembly process requires 9,120 assembly hours and this can be performed by five men working 40 hours per week plus a little overtime.

Assuming labour rates are £12 per hour for normal time, £18 per hour for overtime and that a standard working week is 40 hours over 45 weeks p.a.

The labour cost will be:

Standard hours (5 × 40 × 45) = 9,000 hours @ £12 = £108,000

Overtime hours 120 hours @ £18 = £2,160

Totals 9,120 hours £110,160

The direct labour budget for the assembly plant will, therefore, be:

Labour cost £110,160

Employee numbers 5

A labour budget will be prepared for each production process and, if a standard costing system is used, the labour rates will become the standard rates used. Standard costing systems will be discussed in the chapter on costing.

Any expenditure variances against the labour budget will generally be due either to rate, additional hours or slippage.

The direct materials budget

The direct materials budget will determine how much material or what components are required to produce the production budget volumes. For the assembly process it could look like this:

TABLE 8.7

Component	Qty 3m	Qty 4m	Qty 5m	Qty 6m	Total Qty	Unit cost £	Total cost £
Tubes (metres)	3,060	2,400	1,100	720	7,280	5	36,400
Soles	510	300	110	60	980	40	39,200
Thwarts	510	300	110	60	980	7	6,860
Rope (metres)	4,590	3,600	1,650	1,080	10,920	1.5	16,380
Hulls (metres)	1,530	1,200	550	360	3,640	30	109,200
Glue (litres)	510	400	185	120	1,215	30	36,450
Eyes	510	300	110	60	980	5	4,900
Oars	1,020	600	220	120	1,960	40	74,800
Oar crutches	1,020	600	220	120	1,960	10	19,600
Total							343,790

The total material cost of assembling the production budget requirement is £343,790. The unit costs shown above will form the standard material costs for the period.

Budgeted contribution

We have now completed the sales budget and the direct labour and material budgets for assembly.

Assuming that there was only one other manufacturing process and that the direct labour budget for this was £30,000 and the direct materials budget (paint) was £10,000 then the budgeted contribution (gross profit percentage) would be:

Sales	£1,150,000
Direct labour £110,160 + £30,000	(£140,160)
Direct materials £343,790 + £10,000	(£353,790)
Gross profit	£656,050
Gross Margin % = 656,050/1,150,000	**57%**

This is the gross profit before overheads. It shows the contribution a sale makes after deducting the direct costs towards fixed overhead expenses and profits. Note that most of the direct costs are considered to be variable in that they vary with a level of production. Less production should mean fewer costs.

The gross margin percentage is one of the key 'dashboard' figures in a company and will be carefully monitored each time a sale is made.

Overhead expenditure budgets

Many other departments in a company are not directly involved in the manufacturing or production process but support it in some way. For example, the Human Resources, Finance and Stock Control departments. The costs of running these departments tend not to vary with the level of production in the way that direct costs do. Within a budget period they are either fixed or semi-fixed costs.

These budgets must be prepared on a zero basis by estimating the resources required to deliver the departmental objectives. The cost of these departments may also be compared with the cost of using an outsourced service or a shared service. The previous year's expenditure is usually shown on the budget worksheet as a guide to costs but this should not be used as a fundamental base for the current budget. An example of a typical departmental overhead budget is given below:

TABLE 8.8

Expenditure type	2012 budget	2012 actual	2013 budget	Comments
Salaries	50	51	53	4% increase
Bonuses	5	4	5	10% for on target
Travel	10	1	8	Audit branches
Training	3	2	3	CPE courses
Vehicle exp.	7	6	7	Lease plus running costs
Entertainment	2	1	0	Nothing planned
Office space	7	6	6	Rent, rates, light, heat apportioned
Stationery	4	3	3	Quoted from supplier
Software	2	2	0	No new software planned
IT support	5	4	5	Contracted rate for IT support
Telephone	1	1	1	Annual usage
Temp staff	3	5	3	For possible illness
Totals	**99**	**86**	**94**	

This Finance Department budget supports the following key tasks identified in the plan:

1 Meet statutory obligations to maintain proper accounts and file annual return.
2 Maintain VAT and other taxation records.
3 Pay staff, run payroll, keep NI and PAYE records.
4 Maintain supplier accounts and ensure payments.
5 Maintain debtors ledger and credit control.
6 Prepare product costings.
7 Prepare internal budgets and management accounts.
8 Maintain cash records and bank accounts.
9 Obtain audit clearance.
10 Provide strategic financial advice to the board.

It may be possible to allocate the £94K resource budget across the above 10 tasks in order to compare them with outside costs and outsourced services.

For example, of the £94K budget it might be estimated on a time-apportioned basis that the costs attributable to the payroll task are £15K.

If it is possible to get payroll outsourced at a cost of only £10K then it might be worthwhile considering this. However, as is often the case, by outsourcing payroll the company might not lose the whole of the £15K of internal costs apportioned because staff perform more than one function and cannot be easily separated. However, there might be a case for outsourcing and in any case this type of exercise does highlight inefficiencies. Of course, outsourcing is more than a financial decision. Quality, continuity and a whole lot more factors come into the equation.

The Finance Department costs tend to be fixed or semi-fixed during the budget period. Staff can be laid off but notice periods and redundancy pay may offset or partially offset any savings in the year. However, some other departments may have costs of a more variable nature. For example, the Sales Department's salaries and bonuses may vary with sales levels because sales staff are often paid commissions.

The costs of a department are sometimes allocated to an identified internal customer (another cost centre). The reasoning behind this is that it shows the full costs incurred by a particular department. For example, the Finance Department might allocate payroll management costs to all other departments on the basis of personnel numbers. The method for doing this is internal charging. Some finance directors do not like internal charging because it can become confusing and there is an argument that there is little point in allocating a cost out to a manager if he/she cannot directly control that cost. I mention it here because most companies have some limited form of cost allocation to departments.

Research and development budget

Research costs may be considered under two major classifications:

- Pure research – where there is no specific product yet developed.
- Applied research – where the work is related to the development of a specific product offering.

For the sake of this explanation a product is something that a customer recognizes and might buy!

The accounting and taxation treatments of pure and applied research are different and they need to be accounted for separately.

A research and development budget should show the costs of each project and differentiate between pure and applied research cost as in the following example:

TABLE 8.9

Resource	Total budget	Pure project 1	Pure project 2	Applied project 1
Salaries	90,000	40,000	40,000	10,000
Materials	20,000	10,000	5,000	5,000
Licences	2,000	0	0	2,000
Lab costs	6,000	2,000	2,000	2,000
Totals	**118,000**	**52,000**	**47,000**	**19,000**

Capital budgets

I briefly mentioned capital budgeting earlier in this chapter. We will now explain how the whole capital budgeting process works.

To start I will define capital expenditure, which is sometimes called CAPEX.

Capital expenditure relates to items that are not consumed by the business within the budget period but are used over a number of years. They are items of a permanent nature. Examples of capital expenditure are:

- buildings;
- plant and equipment;
- vehicles;
- improvement to existing assets (but not replacements);
- furniture and fittings of a permanent nature;
- Large mainframe-type computers (generally not PCs).

TABLE 8.10

Project	Q1	Q2	Q3	Q4	Total
Extension to paint shop		30			30
Additional plant capacity	10	10	10	10	40
HGV			140		140
Warehouse in Essex		240			240
Totals	**10**	**280**	**150**	**10**	**450**
Funding:					
5-year-term loan for paint shop and plant					70
Vehicle lease for HGV					140
15-year mortgage for warehouse					240
					450

Expenditure such as software, stationery and materials is not permanent but is consumed within the year and is called revenue expenditure. This sort of expenditure is written off to the profit and loss account each year.

Capital expenditure is not totally consumed within the budget year and is not written off to the profit and loss account. Instead it is shown in the balance sheet as an asset. A portion of capital expenditure may be used within the year and this is the amount by which an asset depreciates. Depreciation is usually calculated by dividing the asset cost by the expected life. The resultant figure will be the figure used for depreciation. This can be done on a straight-line basis or a reducing-balance basis depending on the expected depreciation profile of the asset. For example, an asset costing £10,000 lasting five years with a nil residual value would be depreciated at £2,000 p.a. using the straight-line basis. There are other methods of calculating depreciation, such as the mileage of a vehicle. The point here is that the amount of depreciation calculated is written off to the profit and loss account and the value of the asset in the balance sheet will be reduced by the same amount.

As previously mentioned the taxation treatment for capital expenditure is usually through a system of capital allowances. Therefore, to calculate the taxable profit it is normal to add back accounting depreciation incorporated in the P&L and deduct capital allowance from the accounting profit.

In addition to requiring different accounting treatment capital expenditure requires special approval and sanctioning because it is an investment decision rather than an ongoing operational decision as is the case with operating/revenue expenditure.

Different companies have different processes for capital investment decisions. Probably one of the best methods was that identified by Paul King of Queens College Cambridge. He wrote several papers explaining the decision process where he identified the stages involved in capital investment decisions. Paul King's papers were 'Capital Investment Decisions' 1967 and 'Is the Emphasis on Capital Budgeting Theory Misplaced' 1974. I have not identified any better method so will use his stages below.

The principal stages in capital investment decisions as identified by Paul King are:

FIGURE 8.3 Stages in capital investment decisions

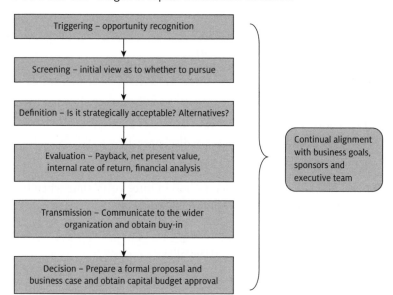

Once a capital budget has been approved by the board the executive responsible for developing the project will normally be required to go back for capital expenditure approval before a final order is placed. Before making a commitment it will be necessary to arrange suitable long-term funds. Capital projects require long-term funds, either loan or equity capital.

Capital rationing

Because capital is often scarce it is not always possible to undertake all of the capital projects in a budget. Choices will have to be made and, all other things being equal, the choices made will seek to maximize overall profits. Projects can be ranked in terms of their net present value (NPV). The NPV is simply the total of the present values of the cash flow of a project.

The present value (PV) of a future value (FV) is:

$$PV = \frac{FV \times 1}{(1+r)^n}$$

Where:

PV = Present value

FV = Future value

r = Compound rate of interest or discount rate

n = the period or number of years

For example, if a project yielded £5,000 in three years' time when the rate of inflation was 5% the present value would be:

$$PV = \frac{£5,000 \times 1}{(1+0.05)^3}$$

$$PV = \frac{£5,000 \times 1}{1.158}$$

$$PV = £5,000 \times 0.864$$

$$PV = £4,318$$

If we have a number of projects that we can invest in but only a limited amount of capital to invest then we will seek to maximize our return by investing in those that produce the highest net present value.

For example, we have £1,900 to invest and there are three project options that produce different returns as follows:

TABLE 8.11

Project	Outlay £	NPV £	Return %
Project 1	500	250	50
Project 2	900	405	45
Project 3	700	266	38
Totals	**2,100**	**921**	**44**

If we assume that the projects have to be completed in total or not at all then we might wish to select Project 2 and Project 3 since this would produce the highest net present value:

TABLE 8.12

Project	Outlay £	NPV £	Return %
Project 2	900	405	45
Project 3	700	266	38
Total	**1,600**	**671**	**42**

By choosing to invest £1,600 of our £1,900 in projects 2 and 3 we would achieve a net present value of £671.

If we have chosen projects 1 and 2 our net present value would only be £655 (£250 = £405). However, we would only have invested £1,400 (£500 + £900) and our return as a percentage would be greater at 47% (655/1400).

So we have choices:

Invest £1,600 in projects 2 and 3 and get a return of 42% to produce a net present value of £671

or

Invest £1,400 in projects 1 and 2 and get a return of 47% to produce a net present value of £655.

Assuming that there were no other investment opportunities and that the projects were not 'divisible' then the company might seek to maximize the net present value even though this produces a lower return on its investment. However, it might decide to invest fewer funds at a greater return percentage thereby keeping its funds intact for potential future opportunities.

Capital rationing decisions can get complicated in large companies with multiple options and the above simple example will give you an idea of the considerations and methods that might be adopted. However, there are often many other factors that need to be taken into account, such as the probability of project returns, which might need to be factored in.

When an organization finds that it is rejecting profitable projects because of limited capital it will, of course, seek to remove those capital constraints. There are many ways of doing this, such as finding a joint venture partner, selling and leasing-back property, improving debts collection, using invoice finance and many more. Some of these options may reduce the return on a project.

Budgeted P&L and B.S. model with test for volume and interest rate sensitivities

The budget model shown in Figure 8.4 shows profit and loss and balance sheet relationships and how budget variables can be changed, one at a time, to test for sensitivities. In this case we have tested for changes in interest rate assumptions.

FIGURE 8.4 Budgeted P&L and balance sheet with sensitivity tests

	A	B	C	D	E	F	G	H	I	J
1	Budgeted P&L & B.S. with test for interest (Case 2) and volume sensitivities (Case 3&4)									
2			Case 1	Case 2	Case 3	Case 4				
3	Interest		10%	15%	10%	10%				
4	Taxation		−25%	−25%	−25%	−25%				
5	**Budgeted P&L**									
6	Sales volume		20	20	30	10				
7	Sales price		£8	£8	£8	£8				
8	Sales budget		£160	£160	£240	£80				
9	Unit material cost		−1	−1	−1	−1				
10	Unit labour cost		−2	−2	−2	−2				
11	Total unit direct costs		−3	−3	−3	−3				
12	Direct costs		−60	−60	−90	−30				
13	Contribution		100	100	150	50				
14	Overheads		−30	−30	−30	−30				
15	Interest		−10	−15	−10	−10				
16	Profit before tax		60	55	110	10				
17	Tax		−15	−14	−28	−3				
18	Profit after tax		45	41	83	8				
19	**Budgeted B.S.**									
20	Net current assets		100	96	138	63				
21	Fixed assets		80	80	80	80				
22	Loans		−100	−100	−100	−100				
23	Retained earnings		−50	−46	−88	−13				
24	Paid-up shares		−30	−30	−30	−30				
25										

Interest rate	10%
Taxation rate	25%
Sales volume	20
Sales price	£8
Sales budget	= C6*C7
Unit material cost	−£1
Unit labour cost	−£2
Total unit direct cost	= SUM(C9:C10)
Direct costs	= C6*C11
Contribution	= C8+C12
Overheads	−£30
Interest	= C22*C3
Profit before tax	= SUM(C13:C15)
Tax	= C16*C4
Profit after tax	= SUM(C16:C17)
Net current assets	£100
Fixed assets	£80
Loans	−£100
Retained earnings	−£50
Paid-up shares	−£30

This simple model shows how major budgets are related and how changes in one or more variables will affect other budgets. For example, a change in budgeted sales volumes will affect the sales budget, total direct costs (production budgets), contribution, profits, interest, taxation, current assets and retained earnings. These can be linked on your budget spreadsheet. For the purpose of clarity in this example the effects of changes in interest or volumes on the timing of cash flows have been ignored. Cash flow modelling will be discussed in a later chapter.

The first case on the sheet assumes an interest rate of 10%. To test for interest rate sensitivity use a second case of 15%. This will change the values of interest, profit before taxation, tax, profit after tax, net current assets and retained earnings = C23−D18+C18.

You can produce Excel charts showing the sensitivity of final profits to changes in any one variable. Simply select the columns to be charted and INSERT CHART. Figure 8.5 shows how profits are sensitive to sales volume.

FIGURE 8.5 Sensitivity of net profit to changes in sales volume

	A	B	C	D	E	F	G	H
1	Sensitivity of net profit after interest and tax to changes in sales volume							
2								
3		Profit £	Sales Vol					
4		8	10					
5		45	20					
6		83	30					
7								

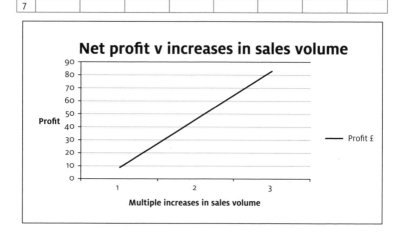

Summary

In this chapter we have discussed how budgets are initiated and support the planning process and how the budget cycle works. We have explained the major types of departmental budget and how they are monitored and controlled together with variance analysis. An explanation of the differences between operating expenditure budgets and capital budgets has been provided as well as the elements of capital rationing.

You should now understand:

- types of departmental operating budgets;
- variance analysis techniques;
- capital budgeting;
- capital rationing issues and solutions;
- the integration of budgets with plans necessary for financial modelling.

This chapter has outlined the relationships between plans and budgets and we will now model each of these in the chapters that follow.

CHAPTER NINE

SALES BUDGETS

Sales budgets and forecasts are key to other budgets

In the previous chapter we briefly discussed sales budgets and explained how other budgets are dependent upon them. They set the course for all other budgets. Just as in navigation, a one-degree error at the start of a long passage will result in an enormous navigational error at the end of the passage! Get the sales budget wrong and resource and production budgets will also be wrong. Because sales budgets are so important it is worthwhile spending a little time discussing them in more depth. Not only are sales budgets vitally important, they are probably the most difficult to prepare because many of the factors involved are beyond the control of the company. Projections might count for little in a sales budget. Every element and assumption needs to be closely examined.

Because a sales budget is so important it normally requires a facilitated workshop led by the sales director with the sales force as participants and contributors. At the workshop territories, prospects, customers, competitors, prices and demand will be examined. Some form of structured workshop using visual and other aids will help pull out ideas and concerns. Sales people, when under pressure, can become surprisingly optimistic but the main purpose of a sales planning workshop is to arrive at a truthful and realistic budget.

Elements of a sales budget

Sales volumes, prices and other factors can all be modelled before a summary sales budget is agreed and fed into the overall budgeting process.

There are many internal and external factors that need to be considered when preparing a sales budget. These will include:

TABLE 9.1

Internal factors	External factors
Growth required	Demand for offerings
Manufacturing capacity	Selling prices (set by the market)
Product costs	Resources
Internal limiting factors	Market conditions
Access to markets and channels	Competitive environment
Logistics, distribution, operational strategies	External limiting factors
Marketing and sales strategies	Access to markets
Sales resources and advertising budgets	New entrants

Product pricing and volumes are largely set by the marketing and sales directors with due consideration to the market. They will need knowledge of demand for their product and competitive offerings. If the market is efficient price may reflect interaction of supply and demand. Supply is determined by the company's and its competitors' ability to offer products. Demand will be determined by both the market's need for and ability to purchase products. The sales and marketing directors will need a deep understanding of their market and their competitor's initiatives. A sales budget summary for a company selling water filters is given below:

FIGURE 9.1 Sales budget 2014

Product	Far East Volume	South America Volume	Total Volume	Unit Price £	Sales Revenue £
20c Filter	100,000	100,000	200,000	3	600,000
30c Filter	100,000	100,000	200,000	4	800,000
40c Filter	30,000	20,000	50,000	5	250,000
50c Filter	10,000	–	10,000	6	60,000
60c Filter	5,000	5,000	10,000	8	80,000
90c Filter	1,000	1,000	2,000	20	40,000
Total					1,830,000

To arrive at the volume and price, estimates will require a critical examination of all the assumptions taken. For example, what information has led you to believe that the market requires certain volumes? What alternatives do prospective customers have? Why should they pay a certain price? Will they continue to have the ability to pay? How will customers find out about your product? Are the channels to market reliable? What are the barriers to entry into the market? Can your company really produce the volume?

These and many other assumptions need to be understood and tested. Excel is ideal for testing scenarios and conducting sensitivity analysis.

Some of the more important assumptions are examined below.

Volume assumptions

The first question to address is why you have selected a particular territory. Do you have reason to believe that this is the best territory or is it just inertia that keeps you there? Typical questions to ask are:

● Why do you have access to the territory?
● What is the potential demand in that territory?
● Can the prospective customers afford your prices?
● What competitive activity will concern you?
● What share of the market will you achieve?
● What are the regulatory constraints?
● What barriers to entry exist?

- What channels can you use?
- How soon will you receive payment?

These seemingly simple questions can be very difficult to answer. For example, there may well be a huge demand for water filters in a developing country but few of the prospective end customers (upon which demand has been based) can afford to pay. This will mean that other agencies will become customers. How will this affect demand, price and cash flow?

When considering volume estimates it is worthwhile asking the question 'Why should a prospective customer want our offering?' Just as a salesperson will 'qualify' a sales lead the whole basis for volume and price estimates needs to be qualified by the sales director and executive team.

Qualification (why)

Qualification is all about asking the question 'why?' Why should a customer want what we have got to offer?

A sales forecast should be qualified to see if it is worthwhile devoting the company's valuable time and effort to attempt winning sales. This is a vital stage that must be undertaken before any sales forecast enters a company's sales budget, which, in effect, will become its sales funnel and pipeline. Many companies express the probability of winning as a percentage and also weight opportunities according to the time that they are likely to take to actually bring on board and become sales. This process enables opportunities to be ranked in order of importance so that business development and other resources can be allocated appropriately. For example, a professional services company might rank its sales opportunities as follows:

TABLE 9.2

Opportunity	Probability	Months to mature	Value £	Ranking
Outsourcing	0.6	12	2m	1
Strategy/Transform	0.4	18	2m	2
Portfolio	0.2	8	1m	3

When determining the probability of a win the most important factor is knowledge of and relationship with the client or prospective customer. Other factors as described above will include competition, client needs and the firm's ability to supply and meet these needs. This last factor is all to do with capability. A seemingly great opportunity will surely have a low probability of a win if it stretches a firm's natural and existing capability. Most firms simply weight the value of an opportunity by multiplying the opportunity value by the probability. The weighted value of the Outsourcing opportunity above would be £1.2m (0.6 × £2m). It is of course possible to apply a further weighting by considering opportunities with a shorter mature date as more favourable. However, the months to mature estimate should perhaps be considered against a firm's resource schedule and it is possible that an opportunity with an urgent need and short close date does not sit favourably with the company's plans and resources.

Once sales volume, price and territory opportunities have been correctly qualified and ranked they can enter the sales budget. As the sales process proceeds and opportunities become better identified their probability of success may increase and they can then enter the actual funnel and eventually the pipeline. However, at this stage we are budgeting at a high level only. Every company has different criteria for what sits in its sales budget, funnel and pipeline.

Strategy (how)

Just as qualification is all about 'why', strategy is all about 'how'. How will we actually develop this opportunity? This needs to be considered at the sales planning stage because if we don't know how to do something we will not do it.

Sales strategy is about developing a win game plan. It is about considering carefully the 'what-if' questions and understanding the sales campaign's sensitivity to the variable factors that will affect it. This includes a sound understanding of the competition and the client's propensity to change its plans. How will the opportunity be controlled and how will risk for the client be managed? How can you convince your client that you will reduce their risks and increase their confidence levels that you will deliver?

When preparing a high-level sales strategy appraise both internal conditions (resources and capabilities) and also the external environment including competitive, legal and economic factors. From this appraisal it will be possible to formulate alternative strategies, evaluate these and select the optimum strategy. This is high-level sales planning from which it will be possible to prepare detailed sales plans against which actual achievement can be monitored and fed back into the original strategy appraisal stage. It is a cyclical process and sales strategy is constantly being reviewed and changed.

Plan

Detailed sales and account plans are prepared from the high-level strategy. These plans will consider what the customer wants and how it will be delivered. A clear understanding of 'what is in it' for each party is essential. A client might want to improve returns on an investment, make cost savings, gain competitive advantage, achieve personal advancement or win any number of unique benefits. It is necessary to understand what these are and to demonstrate in the plan how the provider's offering will achieve these for the client. Then a clear understanding as to what this will actually do for the client needs to be evaluated and documented.

The risks for both parties need to be identified and evaluated in this plan. Then an explanation of how these risks will be managed for both parties should be provided. To convince a client it will be necessary to show that their investment will correlate with their increase in confidence and diminution of risk. This can be achieved through a 'stepping stone' approach where the proposed project is broken down into a number of stages (steps) and the client pays on the completion of each step thereby increasing the control of risk.

The plan should show how resources will be deployed and how the firm will engage with the client during this stepping stone period.

Steps in an account plan for a professional services customer:

- Identify what the client needs both personally and for their company.
- Identify what value there is for the provider.
- Understand what success looks like for the client and for the consulting firm.
- Know what it is you are doing to achieve this success.
- Identify all of the key people in the client firm and understand their powers and motivations.
- Prepare a stakeholder's plan showing what each stakeholder wants and what the provider firm is doing to meet these needs.
- Ensure that your proposal meets the client's various requirements and that it is linked into a current strategy.

- Show the proposal as a series of steps that reach an ultimate goal.
- Ensure that the costs and benefits are identified at each stage and that there are 'break points' at the end of each stage.
- Demonstrate how your approach will reduce the initial risks and increase confidence as each step is completed.

The purpose of these steps is to enable opportunities to be broken down into a number of deliverable stages to de-risk the total sale from both the customer's and the provider's perspective. A sales budget can show how the reduced risks translate into probability and time frames.

FIGURE 9.2 Sales budget, South America

	A	B	C	D	E	F	G	H	I
1	Sales budget – South America								
2									
3		Total mkt	Market	Market		Budget	Unit price	Sales	
4	Product	Volume	Share %	Share	Prob.	volume	£	budget £	
5	20c Filter	250,000	40%	100,000	0.7	70,000	3	210,000	
6	30c Filter	200,000	50%	100,000	0.6	60,000	4	240,000	
7	40c Filter	400,000	5%	20,000	0.9	18,000	5	90,000	
8	50c Filter	100,000	0%	0	0.9	0	6	0	
9	60c Filter	50,000	10%	5,000	0.5	2,500	8	20,000	
10	90c Filter	2,000	50%	1,000	0.5	500	20	10,000	
11	**Totals**	**1,002,000**		**226,000**		**151,000**		**570,000**	
12									

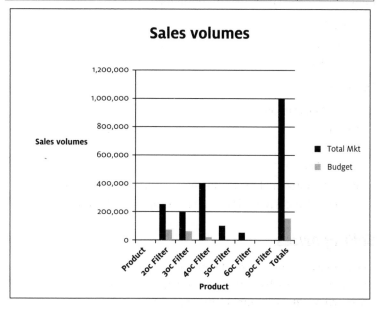

Excel is useful for summarizing and calculating sales budgets. In Figure 9.2 we have shown the total estimated market size; this would have been obtained from market research. Potential market share has been estimated from knowledge of competitor activity. The probability of winning and estimated unit prices obtainable take into account the sales team's knowledge of the territory, the existing customers, agents and prospects. These values have been used to provide a sales budget.

The sheet has been constructed as follows:

Market share column	=B5*C5, =B6*C6, =B7*C7, =B8*C8, =B9*C9, =B10*C10
Budget volume column	=D5*E5, =D6*E6, =D7*E7, =D8*E8, =D9*E9, =D10*E10
Sales budget column	=F5*G5, =F6*G6, =F7*G7, =F8*G8, =F9*G9, =F10*G10
Total mkt volume	=SUM(B5:B10)
Market share	=SUM(D5:D10)
Budget volume	=SUM(F5:F10)
Sale budget	=SUM(H5:H10)

You can prepare any number of graphs. The one shown in Figure 9.2 compares the sales budget by product with the total market volume.

To prepare this graph highlight the Product column, the Total Market Column and the Market Share Column then:

INSERT
CHARTS
COLUMN

To name axis:

Chart Tools (at top of sheet)
Layout
Labels
Axis Titles
Primary Horizontal Axis Title (then use drop down menu)
Primary Vertical Axis Title (then use drop down menu)

Selling prices

Sales prices are, of course, determined by the market. However, it is essential to know what a product costs in order to see if expected selling prices will yield the required level of profit.

For the purpose of this chapter we will define cost and price as being:

Cost = the costs of production and of bringing a product to market

Price = the price that a customer pays for a product or service

Prices tend to be more externally and market focused. Costs are more internally focused although they are affected by external factors. A process for price determination showing how both internal and external factors are related is given below in Figure 9.3.

FIGURE 9.3 A process for price determination

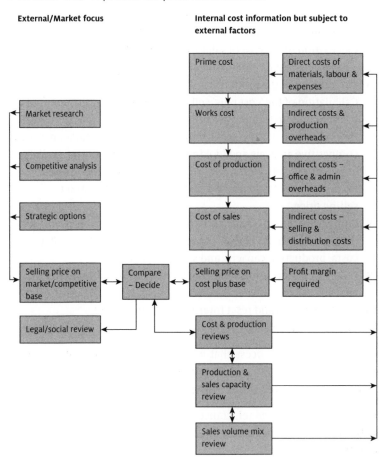

A sales price model can be a useful tool to all sales directors but often it is only the larger organizations than undertake this task. There are potentially many steps involved in price determination and part of the skill is to identify which are important so that the model does not become too complex. Here are some of the steps normally involved in price determination:

1 Production of product prime cost estimates for direct materials, direct labour and direct expenses used in manufacturing the product or in providing the service.
2 Calculation of the works cost, which will include the prime costs plus the indirect costs of production overheads.
3 Calculation of the total cost of production by adding indirect costs of administrative and office overheads to the works cost.
4 Calculation of the cost of sales by adding selling and distribution costs to the cost of production.
5 Deciding upon the profit margin required.
6 Calculation of the 'cost plus' selling price by adding the required profit margin to the cost of sales.
7 Determination of the market selling price through market research, competitive analysis and looking at the strategic options available. Consider marketing strategies – offensive, defensive – and rationalization strategies and factor these into the market selling price.
8 Comparing the externally and internally derived prices. Consider the legal and social aspects of both sets of possible prices. Review costs, production capacity and sales mix options.
9 Feed cost review information back into product costs where appropriate.
10 Review all costs and reset internal prices if feasible.
11 Agree on final selling price.

This is an iterative process that will give the best possible chance of getting the right price to achieve sales targets.

The factors that determine selling prices include:

● customer inertia and reluctance to move;
● the value a customer places upon a relationship;
● time and urgency;
● convenience;
● economic climate;

- perceived quality;
- perceived value;
- unique attributes;
- brand;
- geography;
- competitive strategies;
- marketing strategy – expansion, new market, leader, follower, niches.

The effect of marketing strategies on prices is of interest to us and we will consider them under categories:

- Offensive
- Defensive
- Rationalization.

Offensive strategies

Expansion	Open new branches and channels. **Price to win** new business.
Penetration	Try to win new customers in existing markets and increase/extend existing customer purchases. Differentiation. **Price competitively**.
Challenger	Being innovative and selling new ideas. Seize new opportunities and outsell competitors with quality and **keen prices**. Take on higher risk business at potentially **higher prices**.
Leader	Sell at very keen/**best prices**. Increase distribution network. Increased advertising.

Defensive strategies

Follower	Take lower risks and possibly accept **lower prices**.
Niches	Specialize and perhaps obtain **better prices**.

Rationalization strategies

Cost reduction	Cut costs. Have the ability to sell at **lower prices**.

We can see from the above that whichever strategy is adopted it will have an effect on selling prices.

Pricing strategies are often also considered under the following categories:

Competitive pricing

This is where prices are set with consideration to the competitors' product prices. A product may be totally distinctive, have perishable distinctiveness or have little distinctiveness from the competitors' product. Clearly if there is little that distinguishes your product from the competition's then your price may have to track competitors' prices more closely.

Creaming or skimming

This strategy is often used to gain high profits from early adopters of new products and technology. It involves selling a product at a high price, maybe sacrificing some volume but obtaining high margins and perhaps setting higher price expectations. It may be used in an attempt to recover research and development costs.

This strategy can be used only for a limited time and to win greater market share a seller would use other pricing tactics.

Cost-plus pricing

We have discussed at some depth various costing methods and the need for accurate cost information to see how selling prices will contribute to profits. Cost-plus pricing, where prices are set from costs, may have some use when there is no market information but generally has the significant disadvantage of not taking into account market intelligence.

Loss leader

This is where a product is sold at a low price in order to encourage the sale of other profitable products.

Limit pricing

This is a price set by a company having a monopoly to discourage new entrants into a market. It is illegal in many countries. The monopolistic company sets a low enough price to discourage a new entrant from entering the market.

Market researched pricing

This is where prices are set in accordance with market research data.

Penetration pricing

To help penetrate a market a price may be set at a low level initially.

Price discrimination

This is the practice of setting different prices for the same product in different segments of a market. Examples of this may be age-related pricing or different prices at different times as is often the practice with railways.

Predatory pricing

This is just a term for aggressive pricing to drive out competitors. It might be illegal in some countries.

Premium pricing

Some buyers believe that a high product price equals a high quality. Some sellers will exploit this and price at a premium accordingly.

Contribution margin-based pricing

We have covered this already in some depth in the previous chapters. It is pricing based on the maximization of contribution (selling price less variable cost). It is a method of comparing the contribution that various products make.

Psychological pricing

This is the practice of pricing to have a psychological effect on a buyer. It is believed, for example, that goods priced at £4.99 will sell more volume than if they were priced at £5.00.

Price leadership

The situation where a company is able to take the lead with prices and competitors fall in line and follow.

Dynamic pricing

A mechanism that has the ability to change prices constantly in response to market dynamics and fluctuations. This will normally be carried out using a computer program that tracks competitors' prices and adjusts your own prices accordingly within pre-set parameters. This process is more suitable to fast-moving commodities.

Target pricing

This is a method where a selling price is calculated to provide a specific return for a specific volume of production. The target pricing may be used most by power and utility companies where capital investment is high.

Absorption pricing

This is a method of cost plus pricing that aims to recover all costs attributed to a product on a fully absorbed cost basis plus any possible profit.

High–low pricing

Pricing core products high with lower promotional price offerings to bring customers in when it is hoped they will purchase the high-priced products.

Premium decoy pricing

Setting the price of one product high to make another product seem a bargain. For example, some antique dealers may have a quality item priced very high hoping to make low-value items seem like bargains.

Value-based pricing

This is where a selling price is based on the value to the customer.

Marginal-cost pricing

Selling with consideration to the gross margin. For example, if a product has a total fully absorbed cost of £3 and a variable cost of £2 it may decide to still sell at only £2.50 since this would still make a contribution to the fixed pool of costs of 50p. In other words it is better off with this sale than without it. Of course, ultimately, selling prices need to cover all costs but a contribution is better than nothing at all.

Inertia pricing

Pricing on the basis that existing customers can't be bothered to change or think it is too expensive to change suppliers.

The above factors involved in setting selling prices will all need to be considered. Modelling them using Excel is going to be a time-consuming exercise. Some of the variables are very woolly and difficult to quantify. A pricing model for a large complex organization can take many months to complete and is often adjusted and amended over many years. The danger here is that it can become unwieldy and camouflage many mistakes.

Setting selling prices is one of the most important tasks undertaken by the executive team. It requires a deep knowledge of the external (market) and the internal factors that affect the decision. Once decided upon prices need to be carefully monitored in light of sales results and marketing strategies adopted and model data input updated.

Fixing a selling price is not something that a marketing director can do in isolation. It requires close collaboration between the finance director, the sales director and the marketing director. Understanding the value of a product to a customer and the value of any unique selling points or product differentiation are key and this value information needs to be compared with internal product cost information.

A customer will place a value on a product or services based upon the perceived value to the business, the return that can be made from investing/buying the service, quality, competitive prices and the availability of the product. In the case of some products or services a customer may also place a value on an ongoing relationship with a supplier. An experienced sales or marketing director should know how to maximize selling prices and volumes within a territory and the consequences of expected selling prices not delivering margin expectations will be something that needs to be resolved with the finance director and the executive team. For example, it may be decided that a higher price can be obtained with an investment in marketing or PR.

Market conditions constantly change and the pricing policy needs to provide the flexibility to respond to these changes. This is where marginal cost information can be very useful in order to see what effect a change in selling price has on the contribution to fixed costs and profits. Failure to react quickly and respond to changing market conditions will result in a loss of sales. A sales director needs to have sufficient flexibility in pricing within certain parameters to be able to close deals without having to revert back each time to the executive team each time he/she hits a price problem with a competitor. Sales directors need to know the contribution at different price levels and have the power to negotiate to a degree.

For the purpose of our demonstration pricing model we will consider just three of the most important variables; value to the customer, competitive price; and cost.

FIGURE 9.4 Volume and pricing model

	A	B	C	D	E	F	G	H	I	J
1	Volume and pricing model									
2										
3		Value to		Competitor		Our	Our sales	Our	Competitor	
4	Product	customer	Demand	price	Capacity	price	volume	capacity	sales vol.	
5	20c Filter	£3.20	400,000	£2	200,000	£3	200,000	400,000	200,000	
6	30c Filter	£4.50	300,000	£5	400,000	£4	200,000	200,000	100,000	
7	40c Filter	£6.00	50,000	£6	100,000	£5	50,000	300,000	0	
8	50c Filter	£7.00	30,000	£7	500,000	£6	10,000	10,000	20,000	
9	60c Filter	£8.00	50,000	£7	40,000	£8	10,000	20,000	10,000	
10	90c Filter	£22.00	10,000	£22	15,000	£20	2,000	2,000	8,000	
11										

From the above table we can see the effects of prices on sales volume; for example, in the case of the 20c filter our £3 price will leave us with 200,000 units of unsold capacity. Because the competition can only produce 200,000 units we will be able to meet customer demand not met by the competition and price up close to the £3.20 value to customer level. Our price, therefore, could be greater than £3 and eased up to £3.20. To obtain the additional 200,000 units from the competition we would have to price 200,000 units at less than £2. This might be feasible: it depends upon the contribution and sales mix.

This model shows how we can fulfil a customer's volume and sales needs. It shows, for example, how we can price up when our competitor cannot meet demand. It will also show how much unsold capacity we will be left with if we cannot compete with competitor prices. By setting this up on a spreadsheet the sales director can make price decisions according to changes in customer needs and competitive activity.

The sales mix variance and effect on gross margin

Sometimes a company will believe things are going well when it has a favourable sales variance and sales invoice values are more than expected. However, this might be hiding the fact that the company is selling more of the lower margin products and fewer of the higher margin products. It could in fact have a negative gross margin variance caused by an adverse mix of product sales. This is why measuring the sales mix variance is important. Figure 9.5 demonstrates this:

FIGURE 9.5 Sales mix variance and effect on gross margin

	A	B	C	D	E	F	G
1	Sales mix variance						
2							
3						Gross	
4		Budgeted	Actual	Sales	Gross	margin	
5	Product	sales £	sales £	var £	margin	var £	
6	20c Filter	600,000	650,000	50,000	25%	12,500	
7	30c Filter	800,000	850,000	50,000	35%	17,500	
8	40c Filter	250,000	200,000	−50,000	38%	−19,000	
9	50c Filter	60,000	10,000	−50,000	45%	−22,500	
10	60c Filter	80,000	90,000	10,000	22%	2,200	
11	90c Filter	40,000	30,000	−10,000	25%	−2,500	
12	Totals	1,830,000	1,830,000	0		−11,800	
13							

This company budgeted to sell £1,830,000 and actually sold £1,830,000. Accordingly it had a sales variance of ZERO. However, it was selling more of the lower margin products and fewer of the higher margin products. This resulted in a total adverse gross margin variance of £11,800. A sales variance may be hiding a negative gross margin variance.

Setting up a spreadsheet for the sales mix can be useful when considering the effects of different combinations of product sales on the gross margin and bottom line.

Summary

Sales budgets are key and form a basis upon which other budgets are prepared. When the sales budget has been agreed a company can proceed to prepare a production budget. All other operating and capital budgets that support sales can be aligned to the sales budget.

In this chapter we have considered the elements of sales budgets and how they can be modelled using Excel to establish sales volumes and budgets. Essential elements of a price decision are value to a customer, competitive prices and costs. These elements and other variables can be built into a sales price model that enables a sales director to determine selling prices, volume and sales mix.

CHAPTER TEN

PRODUCTION – MATERIAL, LABOUR AND DIRECT OVERHEAD BUDGETS

Production budget

In the previous chapter I showed how a sales budget is built up. In this chapter I will describe how a production budget is determined and how the resources are calculated to meet production.

The quantity of finished units that will need to be produced to meet the sales budget is:

Required closing stock + sales – opening stock

Therefore, if a manufacturer decided that it needed to carry a stock of finished goods equal to 10% of its sales volume and sales were expected to be 1,200 units when the opening stock at the start of the period was 100 units, then the production required would be:

1,200 + 120 – 100 = 1,220 units

Build up a spreadsheet as shown in Figure 10.1 to show production for each product. The sales column is simply imported from the sales budget and the opening stock will come from the stock records.

Closing stock is 10% × sales.

For product A closing stock = C6*0.1
For product B closing stock = C7*0.1
and so on to product H

Production required is:

Product A =C6+D6−B6
Product B =C7+D7−B7
and so on to product H

You can now see how many units of each product need to be produced and also the total number of units for all products.

The total number of units is 5,530 = SUM(E6:E13)

FIGURE 10.1   Production budget for finished products

	A	B	C	D	E	F
1	Production budget – finished products					
2						
3				Required		
4		Opening		closing	Production	
5	Product	stock	Sales	stock	required	
6	A	100	1200	120	1220	
7	B	50	600	60	610	
8	C	60	600	60	600	
9	D	50	500	50	500	
10	E	30	500	50	520	
11	F	40	1000	100	1060	
12	G	50	600		610	
13	H	30	400	40	410	
14	Total				5530	
15						
16	For example, production required for product A = C6+D6−B6					

Now that we have an overall production budget we can calculate the resources that are needed. For a manufacturing company resources used in the production process can be classified into:

Direct material
Direct labour
Direct overhead

Direct materials budget

This is the budget for direct materials used in the production process. Using the production volumes from the production budget we can now prepare a material budget as set out in Figure 10.2.

FIGURE 10.2 Direct materials budget

	A	B	C	D	E	F	G
1	Direct material budget						
2							
3			Units of	Qty of		Total	
4		Prod.	material	material		material	
5	Product	required	required	required	Unit cost	cost	
6	A	1,220	3	3,660	3.20	11,712	
7	B	610	5	3,050	3.20	9,760	
8	C	600	3	1,800	3.20	5,760	
9	D	500	2	1,000	3.20	3,200	
10	E	520	6	3,120	3.20	9,984	
11	F	1,060	7	7,420	3.20	23,744	
12	G	610	8	4,880	3.20	15,616	
13	H	410	9	3,690	3.20	11,808	
14	Total	5,530		28,620		91,584	

This sheet shows under column C the unit amount of material required for each finished product. For example, product 'A' requires 3 units of material. So, for 1,220 finished 'A' products 3,660 (B6*C6) units of material will be required. If each unit costs £3.20 then the total material cost will be £11,712 (=E6*D6). This calculation is carried out for each row to give a total material budget of £91,584.

If the actual material cost for the volume of production budgeted is different to the budget it will be due to one or both of two possible reasons, either the unit material price was different to £3.20 (giving rise to a material price variance) or the quantities of materials used were different to those budgeted (giving rise to a material usage variance).

Material price variance

= Actual quantity × (actual cost less budgeted cost)

Material usage variance

= (Actual quantity less budgeted quantity) × budgeted rate

If a product requires more than one item of material for its production then you will need a sheet for each material type and a consolidation sheet.

Direct labour budget

Figure 10.3 shows a direct labour budget for an assembly process. Column 'C' lists the hours required to complete each unit. For example, it takes 0.2 hours to complete one unit of product A. The total hours required for A are 244(=B6*C6). The hours can be calculated for each product giving a total of 1,135 hours. If the labour rate is £11.50 per hour then the total labour cost will be £13,035.

FIGURE 10.3 Direct labour budget

	A	B	C	D	E	F	G
1	Direct labour budget – assembly process						
2							
3			Labour	Total	Labour	Total	
4		Prod.	hours per	hours	rate per	labour	
5	Product	required	unit	required	hour	cost	
6	A	1,220	0.20	244	11.50	2,806	
7	B	610	0.20	122	11.50	1,403	
8	C	600	0.10	60	11.50	690	
9	D	500	0.30	150	11.50	1,725	
10	E	520	0.40	208	11.50	2,392	
11	F	1,060	0.10	106	11.50	1,219	
12	G	610	0.20	122	11.50	1,403	
13	H	410	0.30	123	11.50	1,415	
14	Total	5,530		1,135		13,053	

You will need to complete a sheet for each process (assembly, painting, cleaning, packing, etc).

If the actual total labour cost is different to the budget of £13,035 this will be due to:

Labour rate variance
= Actual hours worked × (actual rate less budgeted rate)

Labour efficiency variance
= (Actual hours less budgeted hours) × budgeted labour rate

Direct overhead budget

This will relate to overheads that arise to support the production process. Power, water, cleaning materials, etc. These are all variable costs in that they will vary with the level of production. For the purpose of this exercise we will only consider direct/variable production overheads and shall call these direct overheads. Other overheads that are fixed within the budget period (business rates, insurance, etc) may also be apportioned in part to the production process. However, this is introducing absorption costing into the equation, which does have a place, but not in our example. We are only considering variable costs. The advantage of this is that we can then compare variable costs with selling prices to give a gross margin or contribution towards fixed overheads and profits. We are, therefore, working on a marginal rather than an absorption-costing basis.

FIGURE 10.4 Direct overheads

	A	B	C	D	E	F
1	Direct overhead budget – assembly process					
2						
3			Unit	Total		
4		Prod.	overhead	direct		
5	Product	required	power	overheads		
6	A	1,220	0.50	610		
7	B	610	0.20	122		
8	C	600	0.10	60		
9	D	500	0.20	100		
10	E	520	0.40	208		
11	F	1,060	0.10	106		
12	G	610	0.10	61		
13	H	410	0.30	123		
14	Total	5,530		1,390		
15						

In this case the direct overhead considered is power for the assembly line, which we related to the number of units being processed. It might alternatively have related to assembly hours and the labour budget.

Gross margin and profit budget

This budget shows how much contribution sales have made towards a pool of fixed overheads. Any surplus will be profit. This is done by bringing together the sales and direct/variable costs associated with those sales to arrive at a gross margin. For example:

TABLE 10.1

		£	
Sales		3,050,000	
Variable costs:			
Direct materials	500,000		
Direct labour	700,000		
Direct overheads	200,000	1,400,000	
Gross margin		1,650,000	(54%)
Fixed overheads			
Rents	90,000		
Salaries	800,000		
Other	200,000	1,090,000	
Net profit		560,000	

Note:
The budgeted gross margin is 54%. This is the percentage that the gross margin is to the sales value (1,650,000/3,050,000). This is a key ratio for management to monitor.

Fixed overheads are those that are expected to remain fixed during the budget period and will not vary with the level of production. Direct overheads are those that can be related directly to production processes and in this case will vary with the level of output.

Margin and profit sensitivity

The key elements described above will be modelled on a spreadsheet to show the sensitivity of profits to the following changes against the budget:

Sales	5% favourable
Direct costs	5% favourable
All costs	5% favourable

FIGURE 10.5 Gross margin and profit sensitivity

	A	B	C	D	E	F	H
1	Gross margin and profit sensitivity						
2							
3			Budget	Sales+5%	DC-5%	All cost -5%	
4	Sales		3,050,000	3,202,500	3,050,000	3,050,000	
5	Direct materials		-500,000	-500,000	-475,000	-475,000	
6	Direct labour		-700,000	-700,000	-665,000	-665,000	
7	Direct overheads		-200,000	-200,000	-190,000	-190,000	
8	Gross margin		1,650,000	1,802,500	1,720,000	1,720,000	
9	Rent		-90,000	-90,000	-90,000	-85,500	
10	Salaries		-800,000	-800,000	-800,000	-760,000	
11	Other		-200,000	-200,000	-200,000	-190,000	
12	Net profit		560,000	712,500	630,000	684,500	
13							
14	Gross margin %		54%	56%	56%	56%	
15	Net profit %		18%	22%	21%	22%	
16							

If sales value is 5% favourable against budget the gross margin will increase from £1,650,000 to £1,802,500. This is an increase of £152,500 or 9%. The increase on the bottom line will be the same (£152,500) although it will be an increase in net profit of 27% (152,000/560,000).

Therefore a 5% increase in sales value has provided a massive 27% increase in the bottom line!

If all costs are 5% favourable against budget the increase on the bottom line will be £124,500 or 22%.

It is worth knowing how a budget variance affects the bottom line and having a margin/profit model enables you to do this.

You can also undertake 'What-If Analysis' using the Excel Scenario Manager.

1 Open a worksheet and enter details.

2 Select Data tab. Click What-If Analysis, Scenario Manager.

3 Click Add and then type a scenario name, enter the cell references that you want to change and click OK.

4 Change cells from their initial values as you require.

5 Repeat steps 3 and 4 for each other scenario you wish to consider. Click OK.

6 Select a scenario and click show. This will now display the results on your worksheet.

7 To return to the worksheet select Close.

I find that Scenario Manager is most useful when working with a team using an overhead projector and collaborating. Some modellers simply prefer to just add new columns and change one variable at a time.

Departmental budget spreadsheet

Departmental budgets have been described in Chapter 8. A spreadsheet for departmental budgeting is given in Figure 10.6.

FIGURE 10.6 Departmental budget with variance analysis

	A	B	C	D	E	F	G	H	I
1	Departmental budget with variance analysis								
2	Department:......................				Date:....................				
3	All values are £000s YTD								
4						Variance analysis			
5	Expenditure		Budget	Actual	Variance	Ad.outlay	Rate	Timing	
6	Salaries & wages		200,000	150,000	50,000			50,000	
7	Pension cont.		10,000	7,500	2,500			2,500	
8	Medical benefits		12,000	9,000	3,000			3,000	
9	Travel & subsistence		10,000	2,000	8,000	6,000		2,000	
10	Entertaining		3,000	1,000	2,000	1,000		1,000	
11	Training		5,000	6,000	−1,000	−1,000			
12	Rent		8,000	7,000	1,000		−1,000	2,000	
13	Rates		2,000	1,500	500		−200	700	
14	Power		1,000	1,200	−200		−300	100	
15	Telephone		1,000	900	100		−100	200	
16	Motor		6,000	7,000	−1,000	−1,000			
17	Insurance		1,000	800	200		200		
18	Stationery		500	900	−400	−400			
19	Advertising		2,000	3,000	−1,000	−1,000			
20	Recruitment		5,000	7,000	−2,000	−2,000			
21	Equipment		500	200	300			300	
22	Totals		267,000	205,000	62,000	1,600	−1,400	61,800	
23									

In summary:

TABLE 10.2

	£ooos YTD	
Budget	267,000	
Actual	205,000	
Variance	62,000	
Due to:		
Additional outlay	1,600	(additional purchases/resources)
Rate	–1,400	(inflation/rate increases)
Timing	61,800	(will spend later in the year)
Total	62,000	

A spreadsheet similar to Figure 10.6 can be sent to each manager for completion. Generally, it is simpler and clearer to work in Year To Date (YTD) figures. Reporting current month figures clutters the spreadsheet and it is easier to then make mistakes in variance analysis.

The actual values shown on the sheet may be imported from another source. For example, data may be imported from:

● a Microsoft Access database;
● a web page;
● a text file;
● a SQL Server (import data into Excel as a Table or Pivot Table);
● XML Data Import;
● other sources (go to Data/Get external Data on the spreadsheet bar).

Summary

This chapter has described a spreadsheet layout for production, material, labour, overhead and gross margin budgets. Most CEOs have a few key figures and ratios that they monitor on a daily basis and gross margin will be one of these. All favourable variances are welcome but remember that a 5% increase in sales value is worth more on the bottom line than a 5% reduction in costs. Growth is key since the benefits of cost cutting are limited. When in trouble cost cutting will help in the short term but eventually increased sales value will need to be achieved.

CHAPTER ELEVEN

FIXED ASSETS AND DEPRECIATION

In the previous chapters we have discussed capital budgeting processes. In this chapter we will describe how depreciation is calculated from fixed assets using spreadsheets.

Fixed assets are items that are used in the business for more than one accounting period; for example, motor vehicles and plant are fixed assets. Because fixed assets are used for a number of years it would be wrong to charge the entire cost of the asset against the P&L in the year that it was purchased. What needs to happen is to work out how much of the asset has been used (or how much it has depreciated) during the period of account and charge that amount to the P&L. This charge is called depreciation.

Depreciation may be calculated for accounting purposes or for the tax authorities when it might be referred to as a capital allowance or tax depreciation. Accounting depreciation is calculated in accordance with accounting standards and tax depreciation is calculated in accordance with tax regulations. We will start by describing accounting depreciation.

Accounting depreciation, straight line and reducing balance

There are many methods of calculating accounting depreciation. These include straight line, reducing balance, sum of the digits and revaluation. The two most common methods are straight line and reducing balance and it is these methods that I will describe below. When choosing which method to use refer to the relevant accounting standard in your country of operation and remember the two basic accounting concepts of MATCHING and CONSERVATISM. Match expenditure with income and recognize costs as soon as they are incurred.

Straight line depreciation

Under this method a fixed amount of depreciation is charged over the period of an asset's life. For example, an asset costs £33,000 and has a life of five years. It has a residual value (scrap value) of £3,000. The straight line charge for depreciation will be:

Cost	33,000
Residual value	−3,000
Value to be written down	30,000
Life	5 years
Depreciation p.a.	6,000

During the life of the asset (five years) £6,000 will be charged to depreciation expense each year. Of course, this is not an item that affects cash flow. The accounting entry will be to Debit Depreciation Expense (P&L) and Credit Depreciation Provision Account (B.S). At the end of the five-year period the Depreciation Provision Account in the Balance Sheet will have a balance of £6,000, which will go some way towards the purchase of a replacement asset. Over each of the five years £6,000 has been charged against profits.

FIGURE 11.1 Straight line depreciation

	A	B	C	D	E	F	G	H	I	J
1	Straight line depreciation									
2										
3										
4				Yr 0	Yr 1	Yr 2	Yr 3	Yr 4	Yr 5	
5	Balance sheet									
6	Cost			33,000	33,000	33,000	33,000	33,000	33,000	
7	Residual value								−3,000	
8	Depreciation provision				−6,000	−12,000	−18,000	−24,000	−30,000	
9	Book value			33,000	27,000	21,000	15,000	9,000	0	
10										
11	P&L									
12	Depreciation				6,000	6,000	6,000	6,000	6,000	
13										

The spreadsheet in Figure 11.1 shows the balance sheet value for each of the five years and the P&L charge calculated on a straight line basis:

1 Set up spreadsheet headings.

2 Enter the cost value of £33,000 in years 0 to 5.

3 Enter the residual value in year 5.

4 Insert the formula for Yr 1 straight line depreciation in cell E12 = (D6+I&)/5.

5 Repeat this formula in the cells for YR2 to YR5 in row 12.

6 Insert the formula for the depreciation provision in E8 = E12.

7 Insert the formula in row 8 for YR2 = −E12+−F12.

8 Insert the formula in row 8 for YR3 = −E12+−F12+−G12.

9 Insert the formula in row 8 for YR4 = −E12+−F12+−G12+−H12.

10 Insert the formula in row 8 for YR5 = −E12+−F12+−G12+−H12+−I12.

11 Drag and click 'sigma' (under Home tab, Editing) to give column totals.

12 Use the cell format facility (Home tab, Cells) if you require to change format.

Reducing balance depreciation

Under this method depreciation is calculated on the reducing written down value of an asset. This is best explained by means of an example.

Example

An asset costs £30,000 and has a life of five years. What is the annual depreciation charge assuming 20% p.a. depreciation on a reducing balance basis?

Cost	30,000
Depreciation YR 1 1/5th	6,000
Written down value YR1	24,000
Depreciation YR2 1/5th	4,800
Written down value YR2	19,200
Depreciation YR3 1/5th	3,840
Written down value YR3	15,360
Depreciation YR4 1/5th	3,072
Written down value YR4	12,288
Depreciation YR5 1/5th	2,458
Written down value YR5	9,830

This can be calculated on a spreadsheet as in Figure 11.2.

FIGURE 11.2 Reducing balance depreciation

	A	B	C	D	E	F	G	H	I
1	Reducing balance depreciation								
2									
3			Yr 0	Yr 1	Yr 2	Yr 3	Yr 4	Yr 5	
4	Balance sheet								
5	Cost		30,000	30,000	30,000	30,000	30,000	30,000	
6									
7	Accumulated depn.		0	−6,000	−10,800	−14,640	−17,712	−20,170	
8	Written down val.		30,000	24,000	19,200	15,360	12,288	9,830	
9									
10	P&L								
11	Depreciation exp.		0	6,000	4,800	3,840	3,072	2,458	
12									

1 Set up spreadsheet headings.
2 Enter the cost value in years 0–5.
3 Insert formula for YR1 reducing balance depreciation = C8/5.
4 Enter YR1 accumulated depreciation = −D11.
5 Enter YR2 depreciation = D8/5.
6 Enter YR2 accumulated depreciation = −E11+D7.
7 Enter YR 3 depreciation = E8/5.

8 Enter YR3 accumulated depreciation = –F11+E7.
9 Enter YR4 depreciation = F8/5.
10 Enter YR4 accumulated depreciation = –G11+F7.
11 Enter YR5 depreciation = G8/5.
12 Enter YR5 accumulated depreciation = –H11+G7.

Use the sigma sign (Home tab/Editing) for column totals. Using this method gives a reducing charge for depreciation each year.

Whichever method of depreciation is used will require a final adjustment on the eventual sale and disposal of the asset if it is sold for less than any expected residual value.

Additions and disposals of assets

During an accounting period it is likely that additional assets will be purchased and some assets will be disposed of. The spreadsheet in Figure 11.3 shows how you can handle this. Coding is given below.

FIGURE 11.3 Straight line depreciation with additions and disposals

	A	B	C	D	E	F	G	H
1	Straight line depreciation with additions and disposals							
2	Depreciation p.a.		20%					
3								
4				0	1	2	3	
5	Balance sheet							
6	Assets:							
7	Cost b/f			0	30,000	40,000	10,000	
8	Additions			30,000	10,000			
9	Disposal					–30,000		
10	Cost c/f			30,000	40,000	10,000	10,000	
11								
12	Depreciation Prov:							
13	b/f			0	0	6,000	2,000	
14	Charge for year			0	6,000	8,000	2,000	
15	Disposal			0	0	–12,000		
16	c/f			0	6,000	2,000	4,000	
17								
18	Net book value			30,000	34,000	8,000	6,000	
19								

Assume that a company acquires an asset for £30,000 at the end of year 0. Purchases another asset at the end of year 1 and disposes of the £30,000 asset at the end of year 2. Depreciation is charged on a straight line basis at 20% p.a.

1 Cost b/f YR1 = D10.
2 Cost b/f YR2 = E10.
3 Cost b/f YR3 = F10.
4 Depn. B/f = D16.
5 Depn. b/f = E16.
6 Depn. b/f = F16.
7 Charge for year = D10*C2.
8 Charge for year = E10*C2.
9 Charge for year = F10*C2.
10 Disposal = −E14*F4.

Drag down to highlight a column and use sigma for column totals.

Tax depreciation
(capital allowances in the UK)

Tax authorities have their own rules for allowing depreciation as a tax-deductible expense. In the UK these allowances are called Capital Allowances. In other regimes they may be referred to as Tax Depreciation. In either case it will be necessary to add back any accounting depreciation deducted from profits and then deduct the tax depreciation allowance in order to arrive at a taxable profit. For example:

Accounting profit after depreciation	£470,000
Add back accounting depreciation deducted therein	£30,000
Deduct tax depreciation (capital allowance)	−£45,000
Taxable profit	£455,000

Tax depreciation may take the form of a first year allowance, a writing down allowance or both. The method for calculating these on a spreadsheet is no different to that of accounting depreciation. This may be incorporated in a tax calculation spreadsheet.

Summary

In this chapter we have covered the main methods of calculating accounting and tax depreciation including asset disposals and additions. These are best calculated using spreadsheets. Models for depreciation can get complex in companies with large numbers of assets, disposals and acquisitions. These companies will require extensive modelling. For companies with few assets it may not be worthwhile modelling the level of functionality required by a larger company. The same applies to data and systems integration; avoid unnecessary complexity. Depreciation calculations require input from accounting records and asset registers. Smaller companies may simply use a stand-alone spreadsheet for depreciation calculations.

CHAPTER TWELVE

MANAGING AND MODELLING CASH FLOW AND WORKING CAPITAL

Accrual accounting is a wonderful thing. It makes perfect logical sense. It is the internationally accepted standard and few accountants would propose any form of cash accounting to replace it. However, let's not lose sight of the importance of cash. The saying, which I know you would have heard, 'sales are vanity, profit is sanity, but cash is king', holds true. Cash is the lifeblood of any organization. Many profitable companies have folded through a lack of cash. Overtrading is a common danger and banks can be very fair-weather friends. In this chapter we will explore cash and cash modelling.

The cash flow cycle

Most companies purchase some material, do something with it, pay their staff, add a margin, sell a finished product and then collect some cash. The problem is funding the period between making an initial purchase of material and collecting cash from a customer. Funds may be provided by an investor/proprietor/shareholder or by a lender such as a bank. The more money borrowed from a bank the higher a company will be geared. Ensuring that there is enough cash in the bank to fund operations is a key to business survival and this requires careful financial modelling.

The cash flow cycle is the time it takes for a company to convert initial purchases of raw materials into cash received from customers. For example, the number of days funding for a manufacturing company could look like this:

Purchase of raw materials – cash on delivery	Day 1
Time in warehouse – buffer stock	15 days
Manufacturing and W.I.P. time	5 days
Time in finished warehouse	10 days
Sales order and trade credit taken	60 days
Total funding period	91 days

Funding for this period plus some contingency needs to be built into the cash budget so that a company can continue to trade and meet its obligations. Cash may be considered as a part of working capital. Management of each component part of the working capital cycle is essential to cash flow management. The number of days funding required represents the days that a business has cash tied up and this is expensive so the shorter the period the better.

Profit does not necessarily convert quickly into cash and this needs to be recognized and allowed for in business and financial models.

The working capital cycle is illustrated in Figure 12.1. Each element of this cycle needs to be worked to ensure adequate cash is flowing. Maximum trade credit should be taken without upsetting suppliers and losing discounts, stocks of raw materials should be at an efficient level, work in progress should be as short as possible, finished stocks need to be kept low but at a level that ensures customers demands are met and debtors days need to be minimized. All of this requires a lot of management.

FIGURE 12.1 The working capital cycle

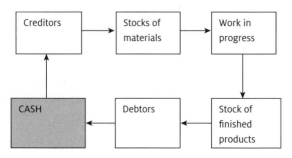

Putting a value on the elements of a working capital cycle will provide a useful indicator of how much working capital is needed for every £1 of sales. We will consider this below.

Working capital ratio

The working capital ratio is an indicator of how much working capital is needed to support sales. It is also an indicator of the efficiency of a company's working capital management.

The ratio is:

$$\text{Working capital ratio} = \frac{\text{Stocks} + \text{Trade Debtors} - \text{Trade Creditors}}{\text{Sales}}$$

Example: Stocks = £400,000, Debtors = £290,000,
Creditors = £210,000, Sales = £2,400,000 p.a.

$$\text{Working capital ratio} = \frac{£400,000 + £290,000 - £210,000}{£2,400,000}$$

Working capital ratio = 0.20

This means that the business needs 20p of working capital for every £1 of sales. If sales were to be increased by £400,000 the company would need an extra £80,000 of working capital (400,000 × 20p). So, before you accept any new order make sure that you have adequate working capital to fulfil it. Many companies overlook this, overtrade and become insolvent. Bank overdrafts (which are repayable on demand) are useful short-term facilities to have in place in order to be able to take advantage of new opportunities.

FIGURE 12.2 Working capital ratio

	A	B	C	D	E	F	G
1	Working capital ratio						
2							
3							
4	Stocks		400,000				
5	Debtors		290,000				
6	Creditors		210,000				
7	Sales		2,400,000	2,800,000	3,000,000	3,500,000	
8							
9	Working cap. ratio		0.2	0.2	0.2	0.2	
10							
11	Total working cap.		480,000	560,000	600,000	700,000	
12							

Codes:

Working capital ratio is: = (C4+C5−C6)/C7
Total working capital = C7*C9
Copy the working capital formula across row 11
Copy working capital ratio across row 9
Insert different sales values across row 7
This will now show the total working capital required at different sales levels assuming that working capital efficiency stays the same as 0.2.

Optimal stock levels

One key factor in cash management is keeping stock at an optimal level. Not too much stock tying up cash but not too little resulting in production delays, customer stress and the potential loss of discounts.

Stocks that are at too high a level will result in:

● excessive stock holding costs (insurance, finance, warehousing);
● deterioration in stock quality;
● obsolescence;
● an unproductive use of investors' funds.

Stocks that are at too low a level will result in:

- high, frequent ordering costs;
- possible loss of quantity discounts;
- a potential failure to meet production and sales requirements.

To strike the correct optimal balance requires the right balance of stock levels and economic order quantities.

Two key figures for efficient stock control are:

- reorder level;
- reorder quantity.

The reorder level is the level at which it is necessary to order more stock to avoid a shortage and obtain best discounts. The reorder quantity is the order quantity that optimizes the variables and constraints of delivery cost, annual demand, stock holding cost and the price per item.

A stock-keeper's record for an item of raw materials could look like this:

Stock item:	China Clay
Stock code:	7691
Reorder level:	5 tons
Reorder quantity:	15 tons
Unit of measure:	Ton

TABLE 12.1

Date	Description	Received	Issued	Balance
1/4/13	Opening balance			30
15/4/13	Issued to production. R53		10	20
3/5/13	Issued to production. R54		10	10
8/5/13	Returned to supplier		5	5
1/6/13	Good received note. GIN 32	15		20
6/6/13	Issued to production. R55		10	10

When stock levels fall to the reorder level (50 tons in this case) an order is placed for more stock. The quantity ordered will be the efficient reorder quantity (15 tons in this case).

The reorder quantity (the economic batch quantity) helps manage stock levels efficiently to ensure that not too much money is tied up in stocks but that there is always enough stock to meet production and sales needs. It is all about achieving an optimal balance.

Economic batch quantity

The economic batch or order quantity (EBQ) is calculated from the following formula:

$$EBQ = \sqrt{\frac{2cd}{ip}}$$

Where:

c = delivery cost per batch

d = annual demand

i = stock holding cost (as a percentage of value or interest)

p = cost price per item

Example

Crates cost £8 each and are ordered in batches of 400. Demand is 5,000 crates p.a. The ordering cost is £50 per batch. The stock carrying costs are 11% p.a. of the cost of a crate. What is the EBQ?

$c = £50$

$d = 5,000$

$i = 11\%$ (or 0.11)

$p = £8$

$$EBQ = \sqrt{\frac{2 \times 50 \times 5,000}{0.11 \times 8}}$$

EBQ = 754 crates

The greater the quantity ordered the lower the ordering costs per crate (unit). However, the greater the quantity ordered the greater the stock holding costs.

Total costs will be minimized by ordering in quantities of 754.

FIGURE 12.3 Economic batch quantity (EBQ)

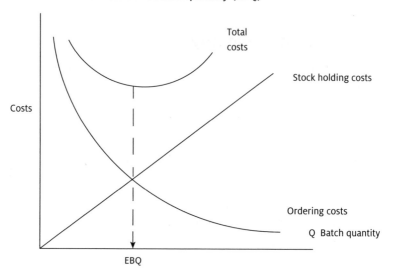

Figure 12.3 shows that the greater the batch size or quantity ordered the lower the delivery costs per crate. However, stock handling costs increase. The optimal economic batch quantity (EBQ) is the point at which the total costs are minimized.

The EBQ or EOQ as it is sometimes referred to can be conveniently calculated using an Excel spreadsheet. Figure 12.4 gives an example using the above figures:

FIGURE 12.4 Economic batch quantity calculations

	A	B	C	D	E	F	G	H
1	Economic batch quantity							
2								
3	Case		D50	D75	D100	D125	D150	
4	c delivery cost		50	75	100	125	150	
5	d annual demand		5000	5000	5000	5000	5000	
6	i stock holding cost		11%	11%	11%	11%	11%	
7	p cost per item		8	8	8	8	8	
8								
9								
10								
11								
12	EBQ		754	923	1066	1192	1306	
13								
14								
15	The coding for EBQ in cell C:12 is = SQRT((2*C4*C5)/(C6*C7))							
16								

Instructions for this are as follows:

1 Populate the sheet:
   - c = £50
   - d = 5,000
   - i= 11%
   - p = £8

2 Insert code in cell C:12 for the EBQ = SQRT((2*C4*C5)/(C6*C7))

You can see that the EBQ shown on the sheet is 754. This has been proven in the formula above.

Copy and paste the EBQ formula code into other columns on the sheet in order to carry out sensitivity analysis. In this case I have shown cases for different delivery costs. For example, if the delivery cost goes up to £75 then the EBQ increases to 923 units.

Once set up you can use your model for different volumes and prices to arrive at an optimal order quantity. Test your model before use by using the EBQ formula to ensure that it is coded correctly.

An added complication is quantity discounts. A quantity discount produces two cost savings and one cost increase.

The savings are:

- fewer delivery costs;
- a lower unit price after the discount.

The cost increase is:

- higher stock holding costs

You can see that a quantity discount is only a benefit if the savings exceed the cost increase of holding the extra stock. To determine whether a quantity discount produces an overall benefit it is a simple matter to run the calculations through a spreadsheet. Compare the total cost using the EBQ with the total cost using the minimum order quantities that qualify for a discount.

Reorder level

This is the level at which a stock item is reordered. It is a level that is high enough to always have enough stock to meet the demands of production but not so high that it ties up more capital than is necessary. The annual demand, lead time, seasonal fluctuations and buffer levels are all factors in determining the reorder level.

The formula for a reorder level is:

$$R = (q \times L) + B$$

Where:

R = reorder level
q = daily demand for an item of stock
L = length of time for an order to be received
B = buffer stock required

FIGURE 12.5 Reorder level for different levels of annual demand

	A	B	C	D	E	F	G	H	I	J	K
1	Reorder level for different levels of annual demand ·										
2											
3	D. Annual demand		7,000	8,000	9,000	10,000	11,000	12,000		7,000	
4	Days p.a.		365	365	365	365	365	365		365	
5	q. daily demand		19	22	25	27	30	33		19	
6	L. Lead time		10	10	10	10	10	10		20	
7	B. Buffer stock		5	5	5	5	5	5		5	
8	R. Reorder level		197	224	252	279	306	334		389	
9											
10	Code for column C:										
11		C:3	Input								
12		C:4	Input								
13		C:5	C3/C4								
14		C:6	Input								
15		C:7	Input								
16		C:8	(C5*C6)+C7								
17											

Example

The demand for bolts is 7,000 p.a. It takes the supplier 10 days to deliver. The buffer stock required to avoid stock run-outs is five.

The stock reorder level is:

$$R = (q \times L) + B$$
$$q = 19.18 \text{ per day } (7,000/365)$$
$$L = 10 \text{ days}$$
$$B = 5 \text{ bolts}$$
$$R = (19.18 \times 10) + 5$$
$$R = 197 \text{ bolts}$$

The reorder level is 197 bolts.

This calculation can easily be carried out on a spreadsheet as shown in Figure 12.5.

Reorder levels have been shown for different levels of annual demand. Using a spreadsheet it is possible to change the value of any variable (cell) and see what effect this has on the reorder level.

In the final column (J) I have shown what happens if the lead time increases from 10 to 20 days. Note that the reorder level doubles!

This is a very simple spreadsheet to set up but it is a very valuable tool as part of stock control and cash management/forecasting.

Debtors

Defining a credit policy and collecting money due from debtors is an essential part of cash and working capital management. A normal financial objective is to keep debtor balances to a minimum so that valuable funds are not tied up but made to work. Another objective of debt collection is to maintain good relationships with customers. These two objectives need not be mutually exclusive. Two objectives of a credit policy must be:

● maximize customer retention and satisfaction;
● minimize debtor balances.

This is primarily about knowing your customers well, building up good relationships and understanding. Understanding your customers also includes credit checking!

Ageing of debtors

Your debtors system should be able to produce a listing of debtors' outstanding invoices by date. See Figure 12.6.

FIGURE 12.6 Aged debtor listing

	A	B	C	D	E	F	G
1	Aged debtor listing						
2							
3			31–60	61–90			
4	Debtor	≤ 30 days	days	days	≥ 91 days	Total	
5	A art ltd	20,000	10,000	10,000	5,000	45,000	
6	A supply	30,000	50,000			80,000	
7	A wheels	16,780	32,450	5,000	2,000	56,230	
8	B bolts	54,000	45,000	16,000	16,000	131,000	
9	B chains	18,000	25,000	2,000	3,000	48,000	
10	B mowers	54,000	27,000			81,000	
11	C Autos	18,000	18,000	9,000	6,000	51,000	
12	D designs	1,600	32,000	2,000	1,000	36,600	
13	D inks	11,000	4,000	200		15,200	
14	E Autos	22,000	5,000	2,000	500	29,500	
15	E paints	33,000	10,000	3,000	200	46,200	
16	Total	278,380	258,450	49,200	33,700	619,730	
17	%	45%	42%	8%	5%		
18	Target	50%	50%	0	0		
19	DSO					33	
20	Daily sales					19,000	
21							

In this example the company had a credit policy with a target of 50% for 0–30 days and 50% for 31–60 days. It did not intend to allow credit beyond 60 days but actually has 13% of its debtor balances more than 61 days old. If the daily sales were £19,000 then the DSO (day sales outstanding) would be 33 days.

Day sales outstanding (DSO)

This is a rule of thumb measure. See Figure 12.6. If total debtors were £619,730 and average daily sales were £19,000 then the DSO would be 33 days.

Cash models

We have discussed the cash flow cycle and working capital efficiency. Clearly we do not want cash in the business not earning profits. We need a safe and optimal cash balance.

Striking the optimal balance might be achieved by using one of the well-known cash management models. We will discuss the Baumol Model and the Miller-Orr Model.

The Baumol Model for optimal cash

$$Q = \sqrt{\frac{2cs}{i}}$$

Where:

Q = total amount of cash to be raised to provide for S

S = cash to be used in each time period

C = cost to obtain new funds

i = interest cost of holding cash

An example of this is given in Figure 12.7.

FIGURE 12.7 Baumol Model for optimal cash

	A	B	C	D	E	F	G
1	**Baumol Model for optimal cash**						
2	Input:	Base case		Case 1	Case 2	Case 3	
3	S	45,000		35,000	45,000	45,000	
4	C	9,000		9,000	11,000	9,000	
5	i	2%		2%	2%	3%	
6	Output:						
7	Q	201,246		177,482	222,486	164,317	
8	n years	4.47		5.07	4.94	3.65	
9							
10	S =	cash to be used in time period					
11	C =	cost to obtain new funds					
12	i =	interest cost of holding cash					
13	Q =	total amount to be raised to provide for S					
14	n =	how often funds should be raised in years					
15							

Example

The AC Lighting company requires £45,000 of cash each year. The fixed cost to obtain new funds is £9,000. The interest cost of new funds is 3% and funds on short-term deposit can earn 1%. How much cash should be raised and how often?

Using the Baumol Model template in Figure 12.7 the optimal amount 'Q' is **£201,246**.

Since the company requires £45,000 cash each year it would raise the £201,246 every **4.47** years.

This model can also be used in conjunction with a 'buffer' amount of cash. It is difficult to predict future year's cash requirements and the cost of holding cash may increase with the amount held. These variable factors can be modelled to test for sensitivity. For example, if the cash required each year reduced to £35,000 then the total amount to be raised would be £177,482 every 5.07 years.

The Miller-Orr Model

In this model the company will buy securities when the cash balance reaches a pre-defined limit. This will lower the cash balance to the 'return point'. If the cash balance falls to a pre-defined lower limit then the company will sell securities thereby increasing the cash balance to the 'return point'. Essentially the Miller-Orr method imposes upper and lower limits that trigger buy or sell actions returning cash balances to an optimal level.

FIGURE 12.8 The Miller-Orr Model

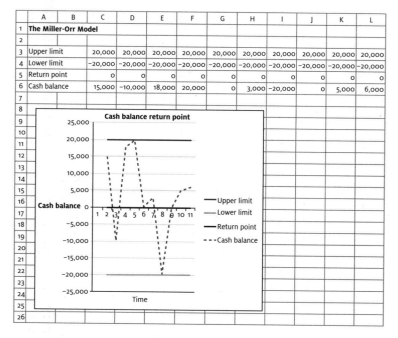

	A	B	C	D	E	F	G	H	I	J	K	L
1	The Miller-Orr Model											
2												
3	Upper limit		20,000	20,000	20,000	20,000	20,000	20,000	20,000	20,000	20,000	20,000
4	Lower limit		−20,000	−20,000	−20,000	−20,000	−20,000	−20,000	−20,000	−20,000	−20,000	−20,000
5	Return point		0	0	0	0	0	0	0	0	0	0
6	Cash balance		15,000	−10,000	18,000	20,000		0	3,000	−20,000	0	5,000	6,000
7												

Cash budget

A cash budget or cash forecast is normally prepared showing receipts and payments for each month. An example is given in Figure 12.9.

FIGURE 12.9 Cash budget

	A / B	1	2	3	4	5	6	7	8	9	10	11	12	Year
1	**Cash budget**													
2	Month													
3	Open Balance	2,000	186,000	200,000	−16,000	200,000	200,000	−16,000	200,000	200,000	−16,000	168,000	200,000	200,000
4	Receipts:													
5	Debtors	1,000,000	1,000,000	1,000,000	1,000,000	1,000,000	1,000,000	1,000,000	1,000,000	1,000,000	1,000,000	1,000,000	1,000,000	12,000,000
6	Cash sales	5,000	5,000	5,000	5,000	5,000	5,000	5,000	5,000	5,000	5,000	5,000	5,000	60,000
7	Sale of asset				300,000									300,000
8	Funding grant ears							500,000						500,000
9	Total receipts	1,005,000	1,005,000	1,005,000	1,305,000	1,005,000	1,005,000	1,505,000	1,005,000	1,005,000	1,005,000	1,005,000	1,005,000	12,860,000
10	Payments:													
11	Creditors	−500,000	−500,000	−500,000	−500,000	−500,000	−500,000	−500,000	−500,000	−500,000	−500,000	−500,000	−500,000	−6,000,000
12	Salaries and wages	−200,000	−200,000	−200,000	−200,000	−200,000	−200,000	−200,000	−200,000	−200,000	−200,000	−200,000	−200,000	−2,400,000
13	Rent	−15,000	−15,000	−15,000	−15,000	−15,000	−15,000	−15,000	−15,000	−15,000	−15,000	−15,000	−15,000	−180,000
14	Business rates	−3,000	−3,000	−3,000	−3,000	−3,000	−3,000	−3,000	−3,000	−3,000	−3,000	−3,000	−3,000	−36,000
15	Building insurance					−12,000								−12,000
16	Car fleet insurance								−6,000					−6,000
17	Corporation tax	−100,000			−100,000			−100,000			−100,000			−400,000
18	VAT			−500,000			−500,000			−500,000			−500,000	−2,000,000
19	Power	−3,000	−3,000	−3,000	−3,000	−3,000	−3,000	−3,000	−3,000	−3,000	−3,000	−3,000	−3,000	−36,000
20	Investments		−270,000	−268,000	−268,000	−272,000		−468,000	−278,000			−252,000		−1,808,000
21	Total payments	−821,000	−991,000	−1,221,000	−1,089,000	−1,005,000	−1,221,000	−1,289,000	−1,005,000	−1,221,000	−821,000	−973,000	−1,221,000	−12,878,000
22	Close balance	186,000	200,000	−16,000	200,000	200,000	−16,000	200,000	200,000	−16,000	168,000	200,000	−16,000	
23														

Opening balance	£2,000
Receipts during the year	£12,860,000
Payment during the year	−£12,878,000
Closing balance	−£16,000

In this model an upper cash limit of £200,000 was set. Whenever the cash balance exceeded £200,000 an investment was made to reduce the balance to £200,000. You can see this occurs in months 2, 4, 5, 7, 8 and 11.

To check that your model is accurate for each month add the total annual receipts to the opening balance and deduct the total annual payments. This should equal the closing balance brought forward each month to month 12.

Summary

In this chapter we have explained the elements of a cash flow cycle and how these can be efficiently managed to help ensure that there is not a surplus or shortage of cash for working capital needs. This has included the control of debtors, day sales outstanding and stock levels. We have shown how stock level can be optimized. Just as stock levels can be optimized so can cash levels and I have explained cash optimization models and in particular the Baumol Model for optimal cash levels. An Excel sheet has been prepared for this and other working capital models. Finally, a cash budget/forecast has been prepared using Excel.

CHAPTER THIRTEEN

INVESTMENT APPRAISAL MODELS

Value is created by investment. Companies invest in order to make a return and governments attempt to promote growth by encouraging investment through both taxation breaks and grants.

This chapter examines how companies decide which investments to make and how to use Excel for modelling the major techniques for investment appraisal.

Organizations make investments with the expectation of gaining future income. Investments may require capital or revenue expenditure. Investment appraisal concerns the evaluation of relevant costs and benefits.

Relevant cash flow

Only costs and income benefits that arise as a consequence of the decision under evaluation are of interest to us when evaluating an investment. Therefore, before we start any detailed analysis of investment opportunities it is necessary to understand what cash flow is relevant in investment appraisal.

Examples of relevant costs are:

- opportunity costs (the cost of a lost opportunity resulting from taking an alternative course);
- incremental costs incurred as a result of undertaking the new investment;

- additional taxation arising from the opportunity;
- additional working capital required to undertake the opportunity;
- additional direct/prime costs;
- additional selling and distribution costs;
- new infrastructure costs;
- additional staff costs;
- any other expenditure arising from the proposed investment.

Examples of relevant benefits are:

- additional sales revenue;
- savings in operating costs;
- income from the sale of assets;
- improved customer retention;
- staff retention;
- existing customers extending business;
- tax breaks and investment grants;
- any other benefits arising from the proposed investment.

Only costs and benefits that are relevant should be taken into account. For example, past costs already incurred are irrelevant.

The following example shows which costs and benefits are relevant to an investment decision.

Example

A manufacturer has the opportunity to buy a new machine for $400,000 to replace an old machine that originally cost $120,000 and has a scrap value of $6,000. The new machine would enable annual production to be 100 units that would sell at $3,000 each.

The production cost of each unit is:

Direct materials	$600
Direct labour	$400
Fixed costs allocated	$500 (Fixed costs do not change with production levels or with the acquisition of a new machine)

The contribution for each unit sale is $2,000 (being $3,000 – $600 – $400).

The new machine has a life of five years and a scrap value after then of $20,000. It also requires additional skilled operatives for 1,000 hours p.a. costing $20 per hour.

The relevant cash flow is:

Year 0	Purchase price	–$400,000
Years 1–5	Contribution 100 units @ $2,000	+$200,000 p.a.
Years 1–5	Skilled operatives 1,000 @ $20	–$20,000 p.a.
Year 5	Scrap value new machine	+20,000
Year 5	Scrap value old machine	+$6,000

It is this relevant cash flow that will be used to appraise the investment. The original cost of the old machine is a past cost and is not relevant to the decision so is just ignored. The benefit of $6,000 for scrapping the old machine has been taken into account since the old machine could have continued to be used.

Pay-back period

This is the most simple and often widely used method of investment appraisal. It simply calculates the time (normally years) that is taken for the opportunity to pay back the initial outlay.

In the above example the initial outlay was $400,000 and there were two relevant scrap values amounting to $26,000. This means that the net outlay was $374,000 ($400,000 – $26,000). The net income from the project is $180,000 p.a. ($200,000 – $20,000). Therefore, the pay-back period will be 2.1 years ($374,000/$180,000). It will take approximately 2 years and 1 month for the returns on the project to pay back the net investment. Since the machines last 5 years this would seem to be a good investment, if the sales volumes are actually achieved.

$$\text{Pay-back period} = \frac{\text{Net investment}}{\text{Benefits}}$$

$$\text{Pay-back period} = \frac{\$374,000}{\$180,000}$$

$$\text{Pay-back period} = \textbf{2.1 years}$$

Pay-back analysis can be used to compare different projects to help decide which one is the best.

An example of an Excel pay-back model is given in Figure 13.1.

FIGURE 13.1 Pay-back period

	A	B	C	D	E	F	G
1	**Pay-back period**						
2							
3	**Inputs:**						
4	Initial outlay		400,000	400,000	400,000	400,000	
5	Scrap values		26,000	26,000	26,000	26,000	
6	Net outlay		374,000	374,000	374,000	374,000	
7	Income p.a.		180,000	120,000	240,000	300,000	
8	**Output:**						
9	Pay-back years		2.1	3.1	1.6	1.2	
10							
11	Codes for pay-back years are:						
12			C6/C7	D6/D7	E6/E7	F6/F7	
13							

The pay-back period for the $400,000 investment is 2.1 years taking into account the relevant costs and benefits. The payback period for alternative income levels is also shown.

Example of the comparative pay-backs for three projects:

TABLE 13.1

	Project 1 $000	Project 2 $000	Project 3 $000
Yr 0 Initial investment	120	120	150
Yr 1 Profits	40	30	30
Yr 2 Profits	40	30	30
Yr 3 Profits	40*	30	30
Yr 4 Profits	5	30*	30
Yr 5 Profits	0	30	30*
Project 1 pay-back period is 3 years Project 2 pay-back period is 4 years Project 3 pay-back period is 5 years			

Purely on the basis of pay-back Project 1 has the advantage.

However, as the pay-back method of appraisal does not take account of cash flows outside of the pay-back period, this is its weakness.

Although Project 1 has the fastest pay-back Project 2 produces a greater profit since its income stream runs longer and the initial outlay is the same.

Pay-back analysis is a useful rule of thumb as long as one is mindful of its weakness and also considers cash flow beyond the pay-back period.

Return on capital

Also know as return on capital employed (ROCE) this method of investment appraisal measures the percentage earned against the cost of an investment.

ROCE is often measured as the percentage of average profits of the average investment.

$$ROCE = \frac{\text{Average profits}}{\text{Average investment}}$$

Example

A company invests $90,000 in a project that has no residual or scrap value at the end of the project. Income is $15,000 p.a. for years 1 to 4 and $10,000 p.a. for years 5 to 10.

$$\text{Average earnings p.a.} = \frac{(4 \times \$15,000) + (6 \times \$10,000)}{10 \text{ years}}$$

Average earnings p.a. = $12,000 p.a.

$$\text{ROCE} = \frac{\$12,000}{\$90,000} \times \frac{100}{1}$$

ROCE = 13.3% p.a.

ROCE can be calculated using several definitions for profits or investments and may use different combinations of these. For example, the calculation can use average profits, total profits, average investments or initial investments. Therefore, when comparing the ROCE of different companies make sure you are comparing a like-with-like method.

ROCE is often used when comparing the return on mutually exclusive projects. A major drawback of the ROCE method is that it does not take account of the timing of cash flows. However, it is a simple and easily understood method that can be used in conjunction with other methods as long as its limitations are understood by users.

Using Excel, as in Figure 13.2, it is easier to see the effect of different return expectations on ROCE.

FIGURE 13.2 Return on capital employed

	A	B	C	D
1	**Return on capital employed**			
2				
3				
4	Investment		**90,000**	
5	Profit Yr	1	15,000	
6	Profit Yr	2	15,000	
7	Profit Yr	3	15,000	
8	Profit Yr	4	15,000	
9	Profit Yr	5	10,000	
10	Profit Yr	6	10,000	
11	Profit Yr	7	10,000	
12	Profit Yr	8	10,000	
13	Profit Yr	9	10,000	
14	Profit Yr	10	10,000	
15	Total profit		120,000	
16	Average profit		12,000	
17	**ROCE**		**13.33%**	
18				

Accounting rate of return (ARR)

The ARR method compares profits after depreciation with the original investment or average net book values. It is expressed as a percentage.

There are several different ways of calculating the ARR and it is important to know how it has been calculated before using the information for comparative purposes.

An example of the formulae is:

$$ARR = \frac{\text{Average annual profit after depreciation}}{\text{Original cost of investment}}$$

A weakness of the ARR is that it does not take into account the timing of cash flows as does the discounted cash flow method, which is explained below.

Discounted cash flow and net present value/internal rate of return

These are the principal and most widely used methods of investment appraisal because they take into account the timing of cash flows. Money changes value over time and the discounted cash flow technique takes account of this. Two methods that use discounted cash flow are the net present value and the internal rate of return. We will explore these methods in this chapter.

Future values

The future value of a project is:

$$FV = PV(1 + r)^n$$

FV = Future value

PV = Present value

r = the compound rate of interest

n = the period

For example, the future value of $3,000 invested for 3 years at a rate of 4% p.a. is:

$$FV = \$3,000 \,(1 + 0.04)^3$$
$$FV = \$3,000 \times 1.125^*$$
$$\mathbf{FV = \$3,375}$$

*(note: 1.125 can also be found in compound interest tables under 3YR/4% (see Appendix 3). It can also be calculated using the y^x key on your financial calculator.)

Therefore, if we invest $3,000 for 3 years @ 4% p.a. it will grow to $3,375.

Present value

Using the above example it is obvious that the present value of the $3,375 must be $3,000. I will now show you how to calculate this.

If the future value is: $FV = PV(1 + r)^n$

then the present value (PV) must be: $PV = FV \dfrac{1}{(1 + r)^n}$

$$PV = \$3{,}375 \times \frac{1}{(1+0.04)^3}$$

$$PV = \$3{,}375 \times \frac{1}{1.125}$$

$$PV = \$3{,}375 \times 0.8889*$$

PV = \$3,000

*(note: 0.8889 can also be derived from discount tables: YR3/4%)

Therefore, the present value of \$3,375 received in 3 years' time when interest/inflation rates are 4% is \$3,000.

You should now understand present value and future value and how to calculate them. Make sure you have a firm grasp of this before moving on to the next paragraph.

Net present value

We have shown above how to calculate the present value. We will now show how to calculate the net present value of a stream of cash flow spread over a number of years. This is best explained by means of a simple example.

Example of net present value calculation

A company has the opportunity to make an investment for \$400,000 in Year 1, which would yield the following income stream:

Year 2	\$150,000
Year 3	\$170,000
Year 4	\$155,000

If the company has a cost of capital of 5% p.a. should it undertake the project?

To answer this question it is necessary to calculate the sum of the present values using the 5% discount factors provided by the discount tables below.

TABLE 13.2

Year	Cash flow $	5% discount factor	Present value $
1	−400,000	0.952	−380,800
2	+150,000	0.907	+136,050
3	+170,000	0.864	+146,880
4	+155,000	0.823	+127,565
		NPV	**+29,695**

To obtain the present value for each year we multiplied the cash flow value by the discount factor (obtained from the discount tables). We then totalled the present value column to give us the net present value (NPV). Since this is a positive figure (+$29,695) the yield provided is greater than the company's cost of capital. Therefore, on the basis of NPV alone, the project should be undertaken.

Had the net present value been a negative figure the project would not have yielded a return greater than the cost of capital and, on the basis of NPV criteria, it would not be undertaken.

The net present value method is one of the most commonly used investment appraisal techniques. Templates are widely available online but make sure that they are from a reliable source before using them.

TABLE 13.3

Years	Discount rates					
	1%	**2%**	**3%**	**4%**	**5%**	**6%**
1	0.990	0.980	0.971	0.962	0.952	0.943
2	0.980	0.961	0.943	0.925	0.907	0.890
3	0.971	0.942	0.915	0.889	0.864	0.840
4	0.961	0.924	0.888	0.855	0.823	0.792

For example, the discount factor in year 2 for a 5% discount rate is 0.907.

The above example assumes that the future income streams are certain. If this was not the case then allowance can be made by reducing the income streams before discounting by their probability factor. For example, if an income stream of $400,000 was only 95% certain to be realized then a value of $380,000 ($400,000 × 95%) might be used.

The NPV function in Excel can save a lot of time!

The code for NPV is: = NPV(5%,−400000,150000,170000,155000)
In Figure 13.3 input the base data into column B.
In cell B9 type in NPV to activate the NPV function within Excel.
Type in the code to show:

    = NPV(5%,−400000,150000,170000,155000)
Don't forget the comma (,) after the percentage sign (everyone does!)
Click off to get the answer: **NPV = $29,743**

This is slightly different from the answer above due to rounding.

FIGURE 13.3 Net present value

	A	B	C	D	E
1	Net present value				
2			5% disc.		
3	Year	Cash flow	factor	PV	
4	1	−400,000	0.952	−380,800	
5	2	150,000	0.907	136,050	
6	3	170,000	0.864	146,880	
7	4	155,000	0.823	127,565	
8		75,000			
9	NPV	**29,473**		**29,695**	
10					

The code for NPV (cell B:9) is:

    = NPV(5%,−400,000,150,000,170,000,155,000).

Note that this produces a slightly different answer from that in cell D:9 where the NPV was calculated using rounded discount factors. The difference is not material.

The internal rate of return (IRR)

The internal rate of return (IRR) is the discount rate which produces a zero net present value (NPV). If the IRR is greater than the company's cost of capital the project should be undertaken using this criteria. The IRR is an easily understood measure but it does not demonstrate the relative size of projects. However, it is widely used as is the payback period.

Calculating the IRR by simple interpolation:

Example

A company has identified an opportunity costing $1,350,000 with the following income stream:

Year	Cash flow
1	+$700,000
2	+$750,000

It has a cost of capital of 3%.

What is the IRR and should the company undertake the project?

Solution:

TABLE 13.4

Year	Cash flow $	4%	PV $	5%	PV $
0	−1,350,000	1.000	−1,350,000	1.000	−1,350,000
1	+700,000	0.962	+673,400	0.952	+666,400
2	+750,000	0.925	+693,750	0.907	+680,250
		NPV	+17,150	NPV	−3,350

Steps:

1 By experimentation find the discount rates that give a positive NPV and a negative NPV when applied to the cash flow. In this case you will find that these are 4% and 5%.
2 4% discount rate gives a NPV of +$17,150.
3 5% discount rate gives a NPV of −$3,350.
4 The internal rate of return must, therefore, lie between 4% and 5%.
5 Using interpolation we can see that a 1% move has resulted in a −$20,500 change in NPV. The move from +$17,150 to −$3,350 is −$20,250.
6 To move from +$17,150 to zero would require the following discount rate:

$$4\% + (5\%-4\%) \times (\$17{,}150/\$20{,}500)$$
$$= 4\% + 0.837$$
$$\textbf{IRR} = \textbf{4.837\%}$$

Proof:

Using the discount rate formula $DR = 1/(1+i)^n$ we have:

TABLE 13.5

Year	Cash flow $	Discount factor 4.837%	PV $000s
1	−1,350,000	1.000	−1,350
2	+700,000	0.954	+668
3	+750,000	0.909	+$682
		NPV	0

A discount rate of 4.837% will produce a zero NPV.

This means that the internal rate of return is 4.837%.

Since the internal rate of return is greater than the company's cost of capital of 3% the project should be undertaken on the basis of this criterion.

(Note: The internal rate of return can also be calculated using a quadratic equation or using a computer programme.)

FIGURE 13.4 Internal rate of return graph

Plot the range of positive and negative NPVs at different costs of capital to determine the point of IRR.

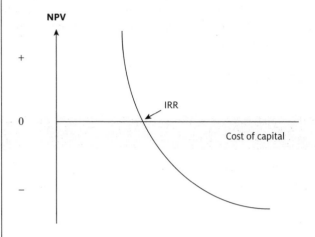

A simple way to calculate the IRR is to use the IRR function in Excel. Type 'IRR' in the cell and then code as shown in Figure 13.5.

FIGURE 13.5 Internal rate of return calculation

	A	B	C	D	E	F
1	**Internal rate of return**					
2						
3	Year	Case 1	Case 2	Case 3	Case 4	
4	1	−80,000	−80,000	−80,000	−80,000	
5	2	13,000	14,000	20,000	30,000	
6	3	17,000	15,000	20,000	20,000	
7	4	20,000	16,000	20,000	15,000	
8	5	22,000	17,000	20,000	10,000	
9	6	28,000	28,000	20,000	10,000	
10	**IRR**	**7%**	**4%**	**8%**	**3%**	
11						

The code for IRR in cell B10 of Figure 13.5 is: = IRR(B4:B9)

Excel is a most valuable, easy to use tool for calculating the IRR of a number of cases.

Capital rationing

A company may have to choose which projects it can undertake within the constraints of its capital and other constraints. Projects may be capable of being only partly completed (divisible) or they may have to be completed in total or not at all (not divisible).

When deciding which projects to complete a company will seek to maximize the overall return subject to the constraints of capital rationing.

Example

A company has three project opportunities (A, B & C). They are divisible and details are listed below. It has $3,000,000 to spend and requires a minimum return of 25%. How should the company prioritize its spend?

TABLE 13.6

	Project A $000s	Project B $000s	Project C $000s
Cost	1,000	2,000	500
NPV	400	1,000	215
NPV as % of cost	40%	50%	43%

All projects exceed the required minimum return of 25%. Clearly projects B and C provide the highest returns and the company will wish to maximize these. Since the projects are divisible the solution will be:

TABLE 13.7

Project priority	Investment $000s	NPV $000s
B	2,000	1,000
C	500	215
A	500	200 (400 × 500/1000)
	3,000	1,415

The company has spread its $3,000,000 across the three divisible projects in the priority of their returns on investment with the highest first to maximize the overall return to $1,415,000.

This is demonstrated in Figure 13.6.

FIGURE 13.6 Capital rationing

	A	B	C	D	E	F	G
1	Capital rationing						
2	000s						
3		Cost	NPV	NPV/Cost	Invest	NPV	
4	A	1,000	400	40%	500	200	
5	B	2,000	1,000	50%	2,000	1,000	
6	C	500	215	43%	500	215	
7		3,500			3,000	**1,415**	
8							

The projects are divisible and the priority will be to maximise the investment in the projects with the higher NPV as a percentage of cost. The maximum NPV subject to the constraint of a $3,000 investment is $1,415.

Had the project not been divisible then the position would be very different.

TABLE 13.8

Project priority	Investment $000s	NPV $000s
B	2,000	1,000
A	1,000	400
	3,000	1,400

Were the projects not divisible the company would maximize its return by choosing projects B and A. This assumes that it wished to use up all of the capital available.

Summary

In this chapter I have shown how to model and calculate some of the principal methods of investment appraisal used by organizations that wish to maximize their return on their investments. The principal techniques include:

- Pay-back period
- Net present value
- Internal rate of return
- Capital rationing analysis.

These are the most frequently used techniques in profit-making organizations. However, not all organizations simply seek to maximize returns on investments. They may be seeking to satisfy a broader range of stakeholders' demands.

In any analysis each variable factor used has a set of underlying assumptions and sensitivities. These may change and in most investment appraisal analysis it is wise to also undertake a sensitivity analysis. As we have previously discussed this is accomplished by taking out one variable factor value and replacing it with another value. Then run the case through again to see what the result is. This can be done a number of times, replacing only one variable at a time in the original appraisal. It is then possible to see how sensitive an analysis finding is to changes in each variable. I have used Excel for this and you can see in the examples how I have saved much time in doing so. For example, calculating the internal rate of return, either by my interpolation or using algebra, takes time and the Excel IRR function saves much time and enables quick and numerous sensitivity tests to be carried out in just a few seconds.

Socio/economic, legal, environmental and numerous other factors apply to all investment decisions in addition to the financial analysis I have described in this chapter. In addition, the effects of taxation should be included in project cash flows.

The methods described are those used most commonly in business investment decision making. For example, we can put a value on cash flows and look at the probability/sensitivity of underlying assumptions and will readily use this information in a 'dashboard' style of approach to management. However, some may argue that this approach is a little blunt in that management teams have options to change things at the start and as they go along. Real option analysis attempts to apply certain option valuation techniques to capital budgeting and, again, Excel is a convenient tool for considering multiple options.

CHAPTER FOURTEEN

THE COST OF CAPITAL

In the previous chapters we have talked about discount rates. In this chapter I will help you choose an appropriate discount rate to use for investment appraisal when using discounted cash flow and net present value techniques. This topic can be a subject that occupies the time of academics who spend a large part of their career debating and arguing about the pros and cons of each method. Certainly it is an important subject particularly for very large organizations making decisions that involve billions. However, I shall try to keep this discussion at a practical level and explain what I think will be useful to a practising business manager and how Excel modelling can make life simple.

The cost of capital is the cost of funds used by an organization. It is the return that an organization gives to its providers of funds and reflects the perceived risk of providing those funds. An organization's capital comes from a variety of sources each of which will have different rights to returns and security. Accordingly each element that makes up the cost of capital carries a different risk and, therefore, has a different cost. We need to consider how these components combine to make up an organization's cost of capital. It is an important element in decision making because the cost of capital can be used as a discount rate in investment appraisal calculations.

First of all we will discus the two concepts of the average cost of capital and the marginal cost of capital.

The average and the marginal costs of capital

The weighted average cost of capital (WACC)

A company has the following sources of capital:

Ordinary shares	£300K @ 10% p.a.
Long-term loans	£150K @ 6% p.a.
Short-term loans	£100K @ 8% p.a.
Total	£550K

Its weighted average cost of capital is:

$$\frac{(300 \times 10) + (150 \times 6) + (100 \times 8)}{550}$$

$$\text{WACC} = \textbf{8.55\% p.a.}$$

Using an Excel spreadsheet as in Figure 14.1 the code for WCC is: = E7/C7
WACC = 8.55% p.a.

FIGURE 14.1 The weighted cost of capital

	A	B	C	D	E	F	G
1	The weighted cost of capital						
2	Inputs:						
3	Source		£K	Rate	Cost £		
4	Ord. shares		300	10%	30		
5	L.T. loans		150	6%	9		
6	S.T. loans		100	8%	8		
7	Totals		550		47		
8	Output:						
9	WCC				8.55%		
10							
11	The weighted cost of capital = total cost of capital/total capital = E7/C7						
12							

The marginal cost of capital

If we assume that this company wishes to borrow more money but the only funds currently available in the market for this level of risk are priced at 12% p.a. then the marginal cost of capital is **12% p.a.**

If additional capital is taken up at this marginal cost then the weighted average cost of capital will increase.

The cost of ordinary share capital

We talked above about the costs of share capital and loan capital. It is easy to determine the cost of loan capital (the agreed rate in the contract) but, what is the actual cost of share capital or equity?

Whilst the directors are under no obligation to make regular dividend payments to ordinary shareholders it must be remembered that ordinary shareholders generally carry the highest risk, own the company and quite rightly expect the highest return. Shareholders will also want to see the market value of their investment maintained or increased. Therefore, the cost of equity is the rate that needs to be paid to maintain shareholder value and to meet their expectations.

Example

A company earns 10p (after interest) per share and pays a regular dividend of 5p per share. The other 5p is kept in the business to help reduce gearing and will earn 5% p.a. The current market value of a share is £1.70.

$$\text{The cost of equity capital (E)} = \frac{\text{Dividend}}{\text{Market value}} \times 100 + \text{growth}$$

or

$$E = \frac{d}{m} \times 100 + g$$

$$E = \frac{5p}{170p} \times 100 + 5\%$$

$$E = 7.94\%$$

The cost of equity capital is **7.94%**.

FIGURE 14.2 Cost of ordinary shares capital

	A	B	C	D	E
1	Cost of ordinary shares capital				
2					
3	Input:				
4	Dividend		5		
5	Market value		170		
6	Growth		0.05		
7	Output:				
8	Cost of equity		7.94%		
9					
10	Code for C8 (COE) = (C4/C5)+C6				
11					

I have kept this simple to illustrate the basic calculation. However, in reality there are other costs associated with raising equity capital. A share issue will require advertising, underwriting, financial and legal advice and other costs. These costs can be estimated and will increase the cost of equity.

Balancing equity and external borrowing

When finding the optimal level of financial gearing a company will wish to maximize the return on shareholders' funds whilst ensuring the financial stability of the company.

As we have discussed in previous chapters, when profits are high a highly geared company may be able to provide a greater return to fewer shareholders. However, when profits are low there might not be much left to distribute to shareholders after paying interest to external providers of finance. A highly geared company may be considered a greater financial risk by both external and new investors thereby raising the cost of capital. On the other hand, equity shareholders carry the greatest risk and will expect the greatest return, which might increase the cost of capital in a low-geared company.

The cost of capital may, therefore, relate to the cost of funds that a company uses taking into consideration the return that investors expect and require. It is the minimum return that a company needs to make in order to pay investors their expected returns. It has been described as the opportunity cost of finance since it is the minimum that investors require for the level of risk they are accepting. If investors do not get this required return they will put their funds elsewhere.

Risk and the cost of capital

The cost of capital will increase as perceived risk increases.

Risk-free rate of return

If there is no risk on an investment, such as government securities, then the rate of return will be the lowest in the market. This is the risk-free rate.

The premium for a business risk

All businesses carry the risk of failure from lower than expected results. There is always uncertainty surrounding business results. Accordingly an investor will require a premium over and above the risk-free rate for making a business investment. This is called the premium for business risk and it will vary between businesses.

The premium for financial risk

Some companies carry a higher level of financial risk. For example, a highly geared company may be more exposed to interest rate increases. Investors will require a higher premium for a higher financial risk.

Elements of the cost of capital

Cost of capital = Risk free rate + Premium for business risk + Premium for financial risk.

Different companies have different capital structures and varying costs of capital.

Methods of determining the cost of equity

If we assume that the market value of a share is related to the expected future dividends from the shares then the cost of providing required dividend growth can be used as a cost of capital. The method used to calculate the cost of equity taking this into account is the 'dividend growth model'.

However, there is a risk in holding shares in a specific company (unsystematic risk) and a further general market risk (systematic risk). An investor may seek to reduce systematic risk through diversification. However, specific unsystematic risk cannot be reduced in this way. The 'capital asset pricing model' is a method that can be used to calculate a cost of equity and incorporate risk.

Capital asset pricing model (CAPM)

This pricing model is used to determine the theoretical price of a security.

The expected return for a security is:

$$E_s = R_f + \beta_s(R_m - R_f)$$

where:

E_s = the expected return for a security

R_f = the expected risk-free return in the market (for example UK government bonds)

β_s = the sensitivity to market risk for the security

R_m = the historical rate of return on the stock market

$(R_m - R_f)$ = the risk-free premium of market assets over risk-free assets.

Example

If the risk-free rate of return is 4% when the average market return is 6% and the sensitivity to market risk is 0.9, what is the expected return from a share?

Expected return   = 4% + 0.9(6% – 4%)

Expected return = 5.8%

Figure 14.3 shows the inputs, code and outputs to calculate the expected return using the capital asset pricing model formula.

FIGURE 14.3 Capital asset pricing model (CAPM)

	A	B	C	D	E
1	Capital asset pricing model (CAPM)				
2					
3	Inputs:				
4	Risk-free rate			4%	
5	Average market return			6%	
6	Sensitivity to market risk			0.9	
7	Output:				
8	Expected return			**5.80%**	
9					

Code for expected return is: = D4 + (D6*(D5 – D4))

Expected return = 5.8%

Significance of the cost of capital

Before you spend too long debating which cost of capital is appropriate to your organization test to see how sensitive the results of a discounted cash flow analysis actually are to the discount rate used. It may be that your own organization's decisions are not enormously sensitive to a discount rate.

Both the dividend growth model and the CAPM methods have their advantages and disadvantages and the finance director will calculate the cost of equity and the overall cost of capital using several methods before deciding which method is appropriate. Generally, these types of debate are more significant to a large company.

Summary

In this chapter I have used Excel to calculate:

- the weighted average cost of capital;
- the cost of equity;
- the expected return using the capital asset pricing model.

The cost of capital is the rate of return that a company has to pay to gain and retain funds from investors who will take into account their risk in investing. It is the opportunity cost of investment capital or the marginal rate of return required by investors. When calculating a weighted average cost of capital in a low-geared company the rate for the cost of equity that is included in the calculation might not be a factor which the overall rate is particularly sensitive to. You need to decide how sensitive investment appraisals are in your own organization to a precise and academically sound cost of capital.

There are arguments for and against each method of calculating the cost of capital. This chapter has discussed some of the principal methods and explained the elements that make up the cost of equity and the cost of capital and it is hoped that you can now decide which method is relevant to your own organization. In a large multinational organization an understanding of the true cost of capital may be considered to be important whilst in a small company it might not be considered to be particularly material to most decisions.

CHAPTER FIFTEEN

BUSINESS VALUATION MODELS

In this chapter we will look at ways of valuing a business and building a business valuation model. There are a number of methods available for business valuations and it is necessary to understand which method is appropriate to the reason for a valuation. Valuing a business is not at all a precise science. Each method will produce a different value and the underlying variables used in any one method may be unreliable. Different buyers will place a different value on a business opportunity depending on how much they can make from the investment. Remember that water might have little value in Scotland but in the desert it can be worth everything.

The purpose of this chapter is not to assist in investment decisions in any way but to discuss some of the methods used to value a business for sale or purchase.

The value of a business and building value

There are many factors that affect the value of a business. Some of these factors are more controllable than others. In broad terms a business would expect to have a greater influence on most internal factors but less influence over external factors. Accordingly, a business that is highly sensitive to many external factors might find it more difficult to ensure a controlled increase in its valuation.

Some of the principal internal and external factors that affect a business value are:

Internal factors

- financial strength;
- quality of executive team;
- quality of staff;
- quality of services and products;
- resources;
- agility and responsiveness;
- customer perception and loyalty;
- efficiency and profitability;
- dividend policy;
- building brand awareness.

External factors

- the economy;
- interest rates;
- political and socio/economic environment;
- supply chain;
- labour supply;
- competition;
- industry;
- foreign exchange rates;
- environmental responsiveness;
- brand acceptance.

A principal objective of most businesses is to increase their value. Value is sensitive to all of the above factors. Accordingly, a business must identify which key internal factors it needs to excel in and how it can position itself in such a way as to minimize its exposure to the largely uncontrollable external factors. For example, developing a strong USP (unique selling proposition) might reduce a company's exposure to competition for a while.

A business should determine which factors affect its value the most and have a plan and strategy to perform well in these. To do this it might carry out a strategic value analysis (SVS). This is a systematic measurement of each part of a business with a view to establishing how it might add value to the business. This will include an examination of core strengths and a comparison with external providers of services that might be outsourced.

Developing a target for a business valuation at a point in time in the future can help focus business strategy. For example, is there an intention to sell the business in the future, to float or go public or is it preferred to keep the company under substantially the same ownership and control? Understanding how the business will be valued is also important. Understanding who you want to value the business and why they should value it is also a key consideration. A quoted company will be valued by the markets with particular attention to its price earnings ratio. However, a company may have other value that is not so easily measured that could greatly affect its future earnings and valuation.

Business value is perhaps linked to the network of internal and external relationships. This is sometimes referred to as a value chain or value network where value is created as a result of collaboration between parts of the network. Company controls and processes are not the only thing that creates value. Understanding the value chain and relationships is key to value creation.

So far in this book we have discussed ways of measuring and improving performance. These are all essential to business success and value creation but so also are relationships and collaborative management of the value chain.

Methods of valuing a business

The economic value of a business is used by buyers and sellers to determine the price they are prepared to buy or sell a business for. It is necessary for all mergers and acquisitions. A business valuation is also used for estate, taxation and a number of other legal purposes.

Before a valuation can be undertaken it is necessary to understand the reasons for the valuation. For example, a valuation of a ship for scrap will be different from its valuation as a cargo carrier.

A value will take account of the price that a willing buyer and a willing seller will agree to. This is called the fair market value (FMV). The market conditions may, however, be far from perfect. For this reason a business valuation will usually start with a contextual evaluation of the economic and industry conditions surrounding the business. Is it a buoyant market or is it in recession? An analysis of the business' financial performance and strength will be compared to the rest of the industry. The valuations placed on competitors will be taken into account.

Common approaches to an initial business valuation are:

● Income/earnings valuations as a going concern.
● Asset valuations as a going concern.
● Break-up asset valuations.
● Market valuations as a going concern.

Each of the above approaches will relate to a particular reason for selling or buying. Often a business will be valued on several bases and the differences between the valuations explained.

Before deciding upon which is the most appropriate valuation method the reason for a valuation will be considered. Possible reasons include:

● The valuation of a company to compare with the offer price of a takeover bid. These can also be compared with the current share price.
● A valuation may be required when a company goes into liquidation.
● A shareholder may require a valuation when wanting to dispose of a significant number of shares that might give a buyer a controlling interest.
● A valuation may be required for bankers when requesting new or additional finance.
● When going public an unquoted company may need a valuation to determine an issue price for its shares.
● Valuations are needed when companies merge.
● Valuations are needed for management buy-outs.
● Loan collateral may require periodic valuations.
● A taxation authority may require a valuation.

Some of the more common methods used for business valuations are:

The book value

This is based on the value of an owner's equity as recorded in the accounts. This may be a starting point but, unfortunately, accounting records may not reflect the true value of assets and liabilities. For example, the Generally Accepted Accounting Practice (GAAP) requires that stocks are valued at the lower of cost or net realizable value. The good reason for this is conservatism. However, at the point of a business sale stocks may be worth a lot more or a lot less than they are recorded in the accounts. It all depends on what value the buyer can derive from the stocks. A buyer may have access to markets whereby the stocks could be converted into cash at a higher price than is recorded in the accounts.

The tangible book value

This method simply values tangible assets and places no value on goodwill or other intangibles. Book values are adjusted by removing intangibles.

The economic book value

This method takes account of all assets including goodwill and values them at the market rate.

Net present value of future earnings

Future earnings are discounted using an appropriate discount rate to give their net present value.

Income capitalization method

This method first of all establishes a capitalization rate that is the rate of return required for the business risk. It then divides earnings using this rate.

Price earning multiple

This is the market price of a company's shares divided by its earnings per share multiplied by the net income.

Dividend capitalization

This is a company's dividend-paying capacity based upon its net income and cash flow.

Sales and profit valuations

Sales and profit multiples may be benchmarked in an industry and used for a valuation basis.

Realizable values

This method determines the net realizable value of assets on a company break-up assumption.

Replacement values

This method estimates the replacement value of a business. For example, how much would it cost a buyer to set up a similar business?

Who can value a business and what information do they require?

A business valuer will need to have a thorough understanding of the industry sector of the business and of each of the disciplines required in the valuation methods. For this reason it is likely to be an accountant, lawyer or a senior banker who has been involved in the sector. Some countries have increasing legislation regarding the sale of real estate including a business and you should check this out with your lawyer in the country of operation/sale.

The information required will depend on the business and the importance of that information within the sector. Essential information will include:

- audited financial statement for most recent and past years;
- financial projections and the basis on which they are made;
- current sales orders and contracts;
- basis of cost estimates;
- supplier contracts and listings;
- aged debtors and creditors listings;
- cash flow statements and forecasts;
- outstanding debts not yet invoiced, accruals, payments in advance, pre-payments;
- basis of stock valuations for raw materials, work in progress and finished goods;
- stocktakes;
- assessment of stock obsolescence;
- property titles;
- land surveys;
- lease and rental agreements;
- loans schedules;
- schedules of investments and securities;
- bank statements and statements for all financial institutions;
- cash book;

- bank reconciliations;
- employment contracts;
- payroll;
- details of directors;
- directors and employee interests;
- organization chart;
- schedule of legal charges;
- debenture documents;
- industry and competitor information;
- list of shareholders, holdings and types of shares.

The precise information and depth of investigation required will depend upon the nature of the valuation and the type of business. The above list is not exhaustive. However, it will give you an idea of the potential areas that need to be covered when arriving at a valuation.

Examples of valuation methods and their appropriateness to valuation reasons

Here we will describe some of the valuation methods mentioned above in a little more detail and discuss how appropriate they are to different situations. Of course, real values are what is actually realized on sale. However, valuations are made without the benefit of a realized selling price and are at best just estimates.

Asset-based valuations

An asset-based valuation may provide a fundamental base and check that can be used to question the results from other valuation methods. They are sometimes referred to as floor values. However, asset-based valuations, just as with other methods, need to consider the premise or reason for the valuation. For example, it is generally accepted accounting practice that stocks should be recorded in the accounts at the lower of cost or net realizable value. However, in a business valuation should they be valued at replacement value, realizable value or scrap value? The answer will depend upon the intentions of the buyer of the business. Does he/she want to carry on as a going concern or is it his/her intention to drop the stock line and sell it off? Or, will stocks just be scrapped? The value will depend upon what use the buyer can put them to.

Example

Fixed assets	£400,000,000
Depreciation	(£200,000,000)
Goodwill	£90,000,000
Current assets – stocks at lower of cost or net realizable value	£30,000,000
Current assets debtors and cash at bank	£80,000,000
Current liabilities	(£100,000,000)
Total net assets	£300,000,000
Deduct goodwill included in the above	£90,000,000
Total tangible assets less current liabilities	£210,000,000
Term loans	(£130,000,000)
Net asset value	£80,000,000
Number of ordinary shares	2,000,000
Net asset value per share	£40

If we deduct the intangible asset of goodwill the net asset value per share is £40. However, goodwill may indeed have a value to a particular buyer or group of buyers. The basis of goodwill valuation will need to be examined to understand its component parts. For example, how much of this goodwill relates to the brand being purchased? Does this have value to the buyer; or, will the buyer be dropping the brand for a more powerful one? How much of the goodwill relates to customers and suppliers and will this have value in the future?

Stocks have been valued in accordance with accounting conventions. However, what is their real value to this particular buyer or to the market the sale is aimed at? Will the stock simply be disposed of at a low price or does it have a higher realizable value to the new buyer?

Fixed assets are in the accounts at a net book value of £200m
(£400m–£200m of depreciation). What is the realizable value of these
assets, what is their value as a going concern, what income can they
generate, what is the current replacement cost, what is their expected
life and what real value are they to the buyer? It could be a different value
from £200m.

At best an asset-based valuation provides a floor value. It can cause
confusion if not analysed, but if it is properly understood in relation to
a buyer's needs it can provide a useful base upon which to consider the
earnings-related valuations, which we will now consider.

Given that the variables in an asset-based valuation may be questioned
it is as well to use an Excel spreadsheet to model a number of different
cases, as is demonstrated in Figure 15.1.

FIGURE 15.1 Asset-based valuation sensitivity

	A	B	C	D	E	F	G	H
1	**Asset-based valuation sensitivity**							
2	000S		Case 1	Case 2	Case 3	Case 4		
3	Fixed assets		£400,000	£400,000	£350,000	£350,000		
4	Depreciation		–£200,000	–£200,000	–£200,000	–£200,000		
5	Goodwill		£90,000	£90,000	£90,000	£90,000		
6	Current assets		£110,000	£90,000	£110,000	£90,000		
7	Current liabilities		–£100,000	–£100,000	–£100,000	–£100,000		
8	Total net assets		£300,000	£280,000	£250,000	£230,000		
9	Deduct goodwill		–£90,000	–£90,000	–£90,000	–£90,000		
10	Net tangible assets		£210,000	£190,000	£160,000	£140,000		
11	Term loans		–£130,000	–£130,000	–£130,000	–£130,000		
12	Net asset value		£80,000	£60,000	£30,000	£10,000		
13	No. of ord. shares		2,000	2,000	2,000	2,000		
14	**Net asset value p.s.**		**£40**	**£30**	**£15**	**£5**		
15								
16	Case 1 = Base case							
17	Case 2 = Stock valuation reduced by £20K							
18	Case 3 = Fixed assets revalued to £350K							
19	Case 4 = Stock valuation reduced by £20K and fixed assets valued at £350K							
20								

Earnings-based valuations

An earnings- or profits-based approach to business valuations enables buyers to understand their possible future return on their investment on the assumptions that the business is a going concern and will continue to make the profits recorded and forecast. These, of course, are two big assumptions in many cases and this is why asset-based valuations are also used to bring valuations back to a more fundamental view.

Two earnings-based valuations are the price earnings method and the earnings yield method.

The price earnings ratio and business valuation

This method uses the following formulae:

$$\text{Market value} = \text{Earnings per share} \times \text{Price Earning Ratio}$$

or

$$\text{MV} = \text{EPS} \times \text{P/E ratio}$$

Where:

$$\text{EPS} = \frac{\text{Profit attributable to ordinary sharesholders}}{\text{Weighted average number of ordinary shares}}$$

$$\text{P/E Ratio} = \frac{\text{Market value}}{\text{Earnings per share}}$$

The earnings yield method

$$\text{Earnings yield} = \frac{\text{Earnings per share}}{\text{Market price per share}} \quad \text{as a \%}$$

$$\text{Market value} = \frac{\text{Earnings}}{\text{Earnings yield}}$$

FIGURE 15.2 Price earnings ratio and business valuation

	A	B	C	D	E	F	G
1	Price earnings ratio and business valuation						
2							
3							
4	Profit attributable to ordinary shareholders:					£500,000	
5	Weighted average number of ordinary shares:					1,000,000	
6	Earnings per share:					£0.50	
7	Price/earnings ratio:					7	
8	**Market value:**					**£3.50**	
9							
10	Market value = PER x EPS					F6*F7	
11							
12	**Earnings yield**					**14.29%**	
13							
14	Earnings yield = EPS/Market Price per share					F6/F8	
15							

Cash flow valuation models

Dividend valuation model

$$\text{Market value (exdiv)} = \frac{\text{Annual dividend expected in perpetuity}}{\text{Shareholder's required rate of return}}$$

There is an assumption in this method that an equilibrium price for a share on the market is the discounted expected future income stream. The expected future annual income stream for a share is the expected future dividend in perpetuity. The equilibrium price is the present value of the future income stream.

Dividend growth model

$$\text{Market value} = \frac{\text{Expected dividend in one years time}}{\text{Shareholder's required rate - growth rate}}$$

Example

The dividend paid by CM plc this year was £400,000. It is expected to grow by 4% p.a. The company's shareholders expect and require a return of 10% p.a. Calculate the value of CM plc using the dividend growth model.

$$MV = \frac{£400,000 \ (1.04)}{0.10}$$

$$MV = £4,160,000$$

Discounted cash flow (DCF) method of valuation

This method simply discounts the expected future cash flow from an investment using the cost of capital after tax as a discount rate. For example, if an investor expects to receive returns of £30,000 p.a. at each of the years 1 to 3 and £40,000 at year 4, when it has a cost of capital after tax of 9% during the entire period, then the value of the investment using the DCF method would be:

TABLE 15.1

Year	Cash flow	9% Discount factor	Present value £
1	£30,000	0.917	27,510
2	£30,000	0.842	25,260
3	£30,000	0.772	23,160
4	£40,000	0.708	28,320
		NPV	**104,250**

Using the discounted cash flow method of valuation the investor would not want to pay more than £104,250 for CM plc.

The value to another investor would be different if they had a different cost of capital.

Figure 15.3 uses Excel for calculating the net present value.

The code for net present value on this spreadsheet is: = NPV(9%,B4,B5,B6,B7).

The small difference between the result using the formula code and discount rate to three decimal places is due to rounding and is not significant.

FIGURE 15.3 DCF method of valuation

	A	B	C	D	E
1	DCF method of valuation				
2					
3	Year	Cash flow £		PV £	
4	1	30,000	0.917	27,510	
5	2	30,000	0.842	25,260	
6	3	30,000	0.772	23,160	
7	4	40,000	0.708	28,320	
8					
9	NPV	104,276		104,250	
10					

Summary

In this chapter we have worked through some of the more popular methods of business valuation. There are other methods that are not so widely used. However, the methods described above are the essential methods that you need to know. At this point, it would be a worthwhile exercise for you to go online and obtain the financial statements and prices for a well-known company and to prepare your own valuation using three methods:

1 the asset-based valuation method;
2 the earnings yield method;
3 the discounted cash flow method.

Go to the landing page of any plc and look for the share price. Then search under Annual Report to find Financial Statements (balance sheet and other statements). Compare the results using different valuations and consider how each valuation might relate to different types of buyer.

In the case of larger listed companies there will be a wealth of market information and prices available to assist in a valuation. This will not be the case for smaller companies where the valuation methods will have less market data to use.

At times market sentiment may influence valuations far more than the underlying fundamentals. During a recession values may become more related to fundamental analysis. Most valuations will use a mixture of income, asset and market information. Valuations often raise more questions than answers! For example, why is the market value of one company much higher than its fundamental asset value compared to similar companies?

Use Excel spreadsheets to arrive at a valuation and in particular the Excel NPV formula code. Look for differences in values using different methods and ask questions as to why these differences exist.

Modellers should be aware that business valuation is not a precise science and that not only are there likely to be large variations in values based on different methods but there may also be large variations in the underlying values and assumptions used in any one method. At best it is a guide that raises questions and seeks explanations for variances.

CHAPTER SIXTEEN

PERFORMANCE INDICATORS

In the previous chapters we have talked a lot about performance measures, ratios and variance analysis. A business executive will have certain key performance indicators (KPIs) that are relevant to his/her area of responsibility and will measure these on a day-by-day basis. Analysing variances against budgets at the end of a month has its uses but by that time it might be too late to take full corrective action. In this chapter we will discuss several systems for measuring performance on a daily basis and how these might be reflected and built into a business model.

Dashboards

Just as the dashboard in your car gives you key information such as speed and fuel level a business dashboard gives an instant view of the key performance indicators (KPIs) that are relevant to an objective or to a business process such as sales, transportation or production. A good business dashboard will let an executive know immediately which areas of business need attention and possibly corrective action. Deciding what are key indicators and ranking them in some form of importance is the first task and the variables we have discussed so far will help you do this. A good dashboard must be simple, uncluttered and focused on what is important. Dashboards in large organizations require a data mining, extraction, cleansing, online analytics and data warehousing capability. The design and data requirements of a dashboard will depend upon what it is to be used for; for example strategic or operational.

When building a business model to experiment with and play out different scenarios it is worthwhile thinking what key performance indicators will be used to control the business so that dashboard indicators can be aligned with the model.

The design of a dashboard can be helped by a good business model that describes how value is generated within a business. The key performance measures highlighted in the process of model building can identify the KPIs for a dashboard.

FIGURE 16.1 Business dashboard

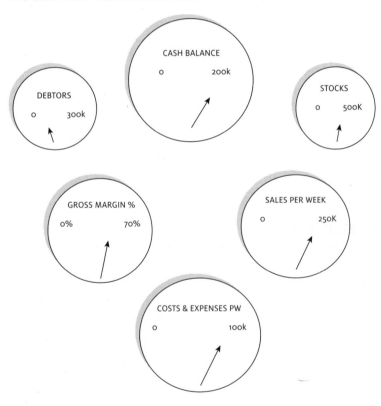

Key performance indicators (KPIs)

In previous chapters we have talked about sales, profits and cash. Clearly these are fundamental measures of performance for most companies. We have explained how a 5% increase in sales might be worth more on the bottom line than a 5% reduction in costs. We have also explained how working capital and cash is vital for business continuance. However, within each of these broad areas reside a number of key business measures that help form the basis of useful KPIs. Each type of organization will have its own unique set of KPIs. A government department's KPIs will be very different from those used by a manufacturing company. Identifying KPIs can be helped by business and financial models.

Stages in identifying KPIs are:

- Building a comprehensive business model.
- Identifying business processes.
- Identifying the requirements for the business processes.
- Identifying the measurement criteria both quantitative/qualitative of the results and their comparison with set standards and targets (standard prices, standard quantities, etc).
- Analysing variances from standards and targets.
- Setting revised standards and targets.

KPIs must be SMART. This means they must be **S**pecific to the purpose of the business, **M**easurable in order to get the real value of the KPI, realistically **A**chievable, **R**elevant to the organization's success and **T**ime limited.

KPIs may be developed for each area of an executive's control, for an entire company and, of course, will vary from one organization to another. Some examples are:

Marketing and sales departments:

- new customers;
- customer retention;
- customer extension;
- new areas of market penetration;
- customer quality measures (ability to pay, introduce or extend business);

- selling prices;
- sales volumes;
- gross margins and profits;
- customer segmentation;
- debt collection;
- customer satisfaction;
- profit margins.

The above marketing and sales KPIs will be identified in a business model and refined in business process development. They may be measured and controlled through a customer relationship management (CRM) system. However, greater integration and embedded complexity does not always lead to greater customer understanding or even communication. In theory it should!

Production, manufacturing departments:

- machine utilization;
- overall capacity utilization;
- material usage;
- material prices;
- labour rates;
- labour efficiency;
- overhead expenditure;
- overhead capacity usage;
- overhead volume efficiency;
- stock levels;
- stock obsolescence;
- finished product rejection
- finished product quality measures;
- just-in-time measures of efficiency.

Most of the above measures are identified in an integrated standard costing system.

A university:

- student satisfaction;
- graduation rate;
- quality of provision;
- employer satisfaction;
- employment rate.

The above indicators are adopted by some governments' use to measure the success and worth of attendance at a university. You might argue that to achieve maximum student satisfaction more students are passed with higher grades leading to a dilution of standards and an eventual reduction in employer satisfaction. Qualitative measures need to be examined in totality with all other measures and not considered in isolation. However, institutions do use certain statistics and qualitative measures in isolation in order to promote their cause. When developing a business model for a university it will become apparent which measures are important to value added and which are necessary to obtain funding. They should be the same but they might be different!

IT department:

- uptime and availability;
- cost compared to industry norms;
- robustness and back-up;
- unplanned stoppages;
- staff retention and development;
- scale ability – ability to grow, develop and support strategic business goals;
- customer satisfaction;
- internal costs compared to outsourced costs;
- vendor satisfaction;
- manageability;
- performance;
- maintenance costs;
- return on IT investment;
- future software support.

Perhaps one of the hardest measures is to identify the return on an IT investment. How many organizations really measure the return on their IT investment?

Suppliers

Business modelling is particularly valuable in explaining a company's supply chain and identifying KPIs for supply chain management (SCM). This will help with just-in-time targets, lean manufacturing objectives, cost control, green issues, fair trade and many other supplier concerns.

SCM KPIs may include:

- lead times;
- logistic measures;
- quality measurement;
- inventory control;
- warehousing;
- procurement measures;
- automated order development;
- integration;
- on-demand ordering and supply;
- automated approval.

Suppliers may want to develop joint KPIs with their customers in order to retain and develop business and have an advantage over their competitors.

Business modelling can help ensure that KPIs are up to date and relevant. In this regard they are useful tools in the creation of a business dashboard. One danger is that once a measure has been developed it can become redundant and irrelevant. Constant updating of a business model will help police KPIs and ensure that they are still needed.

The integrated standard costing system

Having a business and financial model that enables an executive to take control of his/her area of responsibility and to make operational adjustments on a daily basis in order to stay on course is a valuable attribute to any business. The fully integrated standard costing system is one such system and I will describe in some detail how this works and prepare an Excel model to help understand key performance indicators in a manufacturing environment. I have used the word integrated and you will already know my views on the dangers of full integration. However, properly developed and policed an integrated system will produce many advantages including real-time management information.

The fully integrated standard costing system sets standards for costs and these costs are absorbed into product costs. Variances from standards are measured and management actions are taken as a result of understanding variances. It is a form of management by exception.

The cost of a product is explained in terms of materials, labour and overheads and standards are set for these as follows:

Materials	Standard prices	Standard quantities
Labour	Standard rates	Standard times
Overheads	Standard absorption rate (see below)	

The standard absorption rate is based upon the capacity of an overhead facility and the time taken to produce a unit in that facility.

Standards are set annually (or more often) and the costs of products are calculated using these standard costs. The amount of material used, the labour hours and the time taken by the product in the factory will be used in conjunction with the standard rates to calculated unit product costs.

Of course, actual prices, quantities used, labour rates and times taken will be different from the standard rates and variances will be measured. The variances measured under a standard costing system are:

Material price variance – This is the difference between actual prices and standard prices measured over the actual quantity used.

Material usage variance – This is the difference between the actual amount of material used and the standard amount allowed all at the standard price.

Labour rate variance – The difference between actual rates paid and standard labour rates over the actual hours worked.

Labour efficiency variance – The difference between the actual time taken and the standard time allowed at the standard rate of pay.

Overhead budget expenditure variance – A measure of buying efficiency that is the difference between the actual and budgeted overheads.

Overhead efficiency variance – This is the standard time less the actual time at the standard overhead rate. It shows the effect of labour efficiency on overhead absorption.

Overhead volume variance – This is the actual level of activity less the standard level of activity at the standard rate. It shows whether plant is being utilized.

The standard costing system is integrated into the financial accounting system. An example of accounting entries is given below:

Example

A company sets a standard of 20p for a material price.
It purchases 1,000 units at 21p each.
The material price variance will be: 1,000 (21p–20p) or £10 adverse

The standard cost was 1,000 @ 20p	£200
The actual cost was 1,000 @ 21p	£210
The total variance was	£10 adverse

Due to:

Material price	£10 adverse

Using the fully integrated standard costing system the entries in the accounts in respect to the purchase of materials will be:

Debit Materials Account	£200 (with actual quantity purchased @ standard rate)
Debit Material Price Variance Account	£10 (with actual price less standard price × actual quantity)
Credit Supplier Account	£210 (with the goods value on the invoice, 1,000 @ 21p)

As goods pass through the production process into work in progress and eventually into finished stocks entries are made in the accounts at standard rates and allowances. There is no need for you to work through all of these laborious entries since this is a management text and an understanding of reports and accounts presented to you is all that is required. However, the accounting entries are shown in Figure 16.2.

Using the diagram you can track the accounting entries. For example, the raw materials account is debited with the actual quantity of goods purchased at the standard rate and the variance between actual and standard prices using the actual volume is debited or credited to the material price variance. Materials used in production are debited to the work in progress account and the variance between the standard allowance and the actual allowance is debited or credited to the material usage variance account. Labour and overheads are absorbed into work in progress, variances measured and as products are completed they are transferred into the finished stock account at standard rates.

FIGURE 16.2 Fully integrated standard costing system process

Entries in accounts made in accordance with GAAP.
Shaded areas represent accounts.

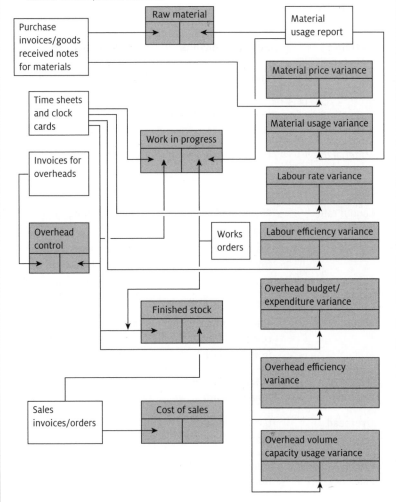

Two of the great benefits of the fully integrated standard costing system are:

1 Integrity of information – it is integrated fully with main financial accounting systems.
2 A dashboard approach that gives management a quick view on areas that need attention.

The type of information produced by a standard costing system and actions that can be taken by management are listed below:

TABLE 16.1

Variance	Possible reasons	Possible actions
Material price	Changes in price Inflation assumptions wrong	Compare alternative suppliers Review budget estimates
Material usage	Using more or less in production	Look for wastage, check controls, review estimates and budgets
Labour rate	Paying staff more or less Staff mix different from standard	Revise costings and budgets If adverse see if a more favourable mix can be achieved. Review budgets
Labour efficiency	Times taken to complete a job different from standard	Measure job times. Review budgets and costs
Overhead expenditure	Actuals different from standard	Review suppliers. Review budgets/costs
Overhead capacity use	Usage standards incorrect	Measure and review capacity
Overhead volume efficiency	Times taken different from standard	Measure job time. Review budgets

The theory is that if standards and assumptions set during the budget process would achieve an acceptable result then by constantly measuring variances from standards and taking remedial actions management stand a better chance of achieving their goals.

However, just a quick glance at this process will demonstrate how it can get complicated and can confuse. Clearly, in a large manufacturing company (a car manufacturer for example) a standard costing system has great value. However, many smaller companies use the system without the resources to ensure accuracy and without the management team to fully appreciate how the system works. For this reason I would suggest that it is more suitable for larger companies. As a manager you may come across this system and I hope that the above has explained the essential process and benefits.

The fully integrated standard costing system that produces valuable live feedback on key variances and performance is integrated with the financial accounting system. A less sophisticated company might produce periodic reports showing a type of variance analysis similar to standard costing reports. Excel is a useful tool for this and data can be imported to the standard costing spreadsheet. For a small company that wants to use standard costing full integration has the usual problems associated with low-cost integration. For this reason a non-integrated approach may suffice.

Sales variances

Figure 16.3 shows how sales variances can be analysed.

FIGURE 16.3 Standard costing system report – sales variances – market share

	A	B	C	D	E	F	G	H	I
1	Standard costing system report – sales variances – market share								
2	Budget v Actual								
3		Std. price	Std. vol	Budget	Act. price	Act. vol	Actual	Variances	Market size
4	Sales A	£5	200,000	£1,000,000	£6	100,000	£600,000	£400,000	700,000
5	Sales B	£7	200,000	£1,400,000	£6	300,000	£1,800,000	–£400,000	600,000
6				£2,400,000			£2,400,000	£0	
7									
8									
9	Variance analysis:								
10			Variances						
11	Sales volume		£200,000						
12	Sales price		–£200,000						
13	Total		£0						
14									
15	Market share:								
16			Budget	Actual					
17	A	28.57%	14.29%						
18	B	33.33%	50.00%						

The codes for sales variances are:

$$\text{Sales price} = ((E4 - B4)*F4((E5 - B5)*F5)$$

$$\text{Sales volume} = ((F4 - C4)*B4) + ((F5 - C5)*B5)$$

This high-level report will tell the sales director what overall sales price and volume variances are. Further analysis can be undertaken to show the effect of the sales mix on gross margins and profits.

Three of the key performance indicators for a sales director that are produced by a costing system are:

Selling prices
Sales volumes
Sales mix (affect on margins)

Other indicators will include:

Market share
Market segmentation

Supporting these indicators will be more qualitative measures including customer satisfaction.

Manufacturing variances

These are:

Material price and usage
Labour rate and efficiency
Overhead expenditure, capacity usage and volume efficiency

Figure 16.4 is an example of standard costing variance analysis.

FIGURE 16.4 Standard costing variances

	A	B	C	D	E	F	G	H	I	J	K	L
1	Standard costing variances											
2	Product: Clay pot 15cm											
3			Standard	Standard	Actual	Actual	Actual					
4			unit price	unit qty	unit price	unit qty	volume	Budget	Actual	Variance	MPV	MUV
5	Material		£5	0.1	£6	0.15	1,000	£500	£900	−£400	−£150	−£250
6												
7			Standard	Standard	Actual	Actual	Actual					
8			Lab. Rate	Unit time	Lab. Rate	Time	Volume	Budget	Actual	Variance	LRV	LEV
9	Labour		£7	0.2	£8	0.3	1,000	£1,400	£2,400	−£1,000	−£300	−£700
10												
11			Stnd Ohd	Standard	Actual	Actual	Actual					
12			abs rate	unit time	exp rate	Time	Volume	Budget	Actual	Variance	OEE	OV
13	Overhead		£9	0.2	£10	0.3	1,000	£1,800	£3,000	−£1,200	−£900	−£300

The codes for Figure 16.4 are as follows:

TABLE 16.2

Variance	Code
Material price (MPV)	=(G5*F5)*(C5−E5)
Material usage variance (MUV)	=G5*((D5−F5)*C5)
Labour rate variance (LRV)	=(C9−E9)*G9*F9
Labour efficiency variance (LEV)	=(D9−F9)*G9*C9
Overhead efficiency variance (OEE)	=(D13−F13)*G13*C13
Overhead volume variance (OVV)	=(C13−E13)*G13*F13

If input values are imported from mainstream accounts then the production director can be informed of variances on a daily basis and take corrective action or amend budgets and plans.

In summary, material variances are due to price or usage, labour variances are due to rate or efficiency and overhead variances must be due to expenditure, efficiency or capacity usage.

Measuring performance by variances from pre-set standards on a daily or weekly basis gives the production director control as long as the system and any integration can be relied upon. The example we have given is for just one component in one product. For a company with 30 products each with 50 components (not unusual) the above information would be multiplied by a factor of 1,500 times. Some form of consolidation would be required to enable effective concentration on key items.

Activity-based costing (ABC)

Activity-based costing assigns costs to activities and then to products. It is, therefore, another technique for allocating indirect costs to products.

A traditional costing method usually assigns overhead costs to products based on an average absorption rate. ABC first of all assigns indirect costs to activities and then assigns the costs to products based on the products' usage of the activities. ABC attempts to identify cause-and-effect relationships in order to accurately allocate costs to products.

It is a system that attempts to trace indirect costs to products by allocating indirect costs to activities and then to products based on their usage of the activities. ABC is useful when indirect cost allocation accuracy is important and when indirect costs are a large proportion of total costs. ABC is commonly used in the manufacturing sector.

The four steps in the activity-based costing process are:

1 Recognize and list the activities in the value chain related to the production process of the product.
2 Estimate a total cost for each of the activities listed above.
3 Compute a cost-driver rate for each activity based on an allocation method that has a direct link to the cost of the activity. See example below.
4 Apply these activity costs to products using the cost-driver rate.

Example

A company classifies paint-room maintenance as an indirect cost activity for the metal lampshades it manufactures. The company estimates paint-room maintenance costs to be £3,000 per month and determines that batches of lampshades sprayed in the paint room are an appropriate cost-driver allocation base for paint-room costs. The paint room produces 750 batches per month. Thus, the cost-driver rate would be £3,000/750, or £3.00 per batch. Therefore, the company would apply £3.00 of indirect cost for each batch produced by the paint room.

Activity-based costing is often used as an aid to strategic decisions concerning processes, outsourcing and selling prices.

Summary

Business and financial models can be constructed to focus on key performance indicators. In this chapter we have shown how to identify key performance indicators for use in a dashboard approach to executive control. To provide daily information that an executive can use to steer his/her operations in the right direction or to make alternative plans requires a certain level of integration. We have shown some of the key performance indicators using the standard costing system as an example and how this can be built in to an Excel spreadsheet.

CHAPTER SEVENTEEN

MODELLING THE COMPANY BALANCE SHEET, P&L AND RATIO ANALYSIS

In this chapter we will show how to prepare a budgeted balance sheet, P&L statement and ratio analysis. Your accountant will prepare full accounts in accordance with GAAP (Generally Accepted Accounting Practice) and with the accounting standards appropriate to the regime of operation. The purpose of this chapter is to enable data extraction from the ledgers so that key ratios can be used as an executive guide.

Prepare an Excel model

Prepare an Excel model similar to that shown in Figure 17.1. I have kept this model as simple as possible to demonstrate the principals. Your own company model will no doubt have more lines of information.

1   Import input data from the ledger. This will be from a trial balance, which is a list of account balances with their values. Check on the spreadsheet that this totals zero.
2   Insert formulae in cells for the P&L output (these are shown below).
3   Insert formulae in cells for the B.S. output (these are shown below).
4   Insert formulae in cells for the ratios that you require (these are shown below).

Example

The general ledger extract from a company has given the following trial balance:

TABLE 17.1

Account	£
Cash	2,600
Stock	100
Cost of sales	100
Expenses	800
Plant and equipment	900
Depreciation expense	100
Debtors	90
Total debit balances	**4,690**
Capital account	−3,090
Bank loan	−600
Sales	−900
Depreciation provision	−100
Total credit balances	**−4,690**

Import the above trial balance values from the ledger as input data onto the spreadsheet.

FIGURE 17.1 Balance sheet, P&L and ratios

	A	B	C	D	E	F	G	H
1	**Balance sheet, P&L and ratios**							
2	**Input = Trial balance from ledger:**							
3	Cash		2,600					
4	Stock		100					
5	Cost of sales		100					
6	Expenses		800					
7	Plant & equipment		900					
8	Depreciation exp.		100					
9	Debtors		90					
10	Capital account		−3,090					
11	Bank loan		−600					
12	Sales		−900					
13	Depreciation prov.		−100					
14	Total		0					
15	**Output = P&L**							
16	Sales		−900					
17	Cost of sales		100					
18	Gross margin		−800		Gross Margin %		89%	
19	Expenses		800					
20	Depreciation exp.		100					
21	Net (profit) loss		100		Net Profit %		−11%	
22	**Output = B.S.**							
23	Capital account		−3,090		Return on capital		−3%	
24	P&L account		100					
25	Bank loan s/t		−600		Gearing %		20%	
26	Plant & equipment		900					
27	Depreciation prov.		−100					
28	Debtors		90		Debtors days		37	days
29	Stock		100		Stock turnover		1	times
30	Cash		2,600		Current ratio		4.65	times
31	Total check		0					
32								

The coding for the balance sheet, profit and loss statement and ratios is given in the table below:

TABLE 17.2

Output description	Code on spreadsheet	Output
P&L:		
Sales	=C12	−900
Cost of sales	=C5	100
Gross margin	=SUM(C16:C17)	−800
Expenses	=C6	800
Depreciation expenses	=C8	100
Net profit or loss	=SUM(C18:C20)	100
Balance sheet:		
Capital account	=C10	−3,090
P&L account	=C12	100
Bank loan – short term	=C11	−600
Plant & equipment	=C7	900
Depreciation provision	=C13	−100
Debtors	=C9	90
Stock	=C4	100
Cash	=C3	2,600
Total check	=SUM(C23:C30)	0
Ratios:		
Gross margin	=C18/C16	89%
Net profit %	=C21/C16	−11%
Return on capital	=C21/(C23+C24)	−3%
Gearing %	=C25/(C23+C24)	20%
Debtors days	=(C28*365)/−C16	37 days
Stock turnover	=C17/C29	1 times
Current ratio	=(C30+C29+C28)/−C25	4.65 times

Note that on the spreadsheet credit balances are show as '−' (negative). For example, sales are shown as −900 and capital is shown as −3,090. If you have trouble understanding the double entry system then I suggest *Financial Management for the Non-Financial Manager*, Kogan Page, 2012 (Chapter 3).

Using the template in Figure 17.1 will enable you to quickly determine key ratios, which are based upon financial data imported from mainstream accounts. You can also use a model such as this for budgeting purposes in order to test out the effect of different plans on basic balance sheet, profit and loss and ratio analysis. In this regard you might want to introduce the effects of taxation and interest into your model. Interest will depend on the amount of borrowing required, which in turn is affected by cash balances (refer to cash forecasting) and taxation will depend upon profits after interest. It is an iterative process ideal for Excel modelling.

Taking a quick look at the ratios in the above example you might conclude that:

- gross margins looks good;
- gearing looks healthy;
- current ratio looks good;
- debtors' days acceptable;
- stock turnover poor;
- net loss not acceptable – perhaps expenses are too high.

However, this may be too simplistic an analysis. How does the gross margin stack up against the competition? What type of stock is it? Are expenses too high? Ratios rarely provide direct answers but they lead a good analyst to ask the right questions.

A more comprehensive example of ratio analysis is given below.

Analysis and financial ratios

In the previous paragraph we covered the basics of preparing a profit and loss statement, balance sheet and ratio analysis using an Excel spreadsheet. We will now examine more completed financial statements and show how they can be used to analyse performance. We will also cover the essential ratios that are used to provide a guide to business performance.

Below is an example of a typical profit and loss account (Table 17.3) and balance sheet (Table 17.4) for a medium-sized company. We will use these financial statements for further analysis. A full set of published accounts will contain considerably more information to comply with GAAP and various accounting standards. However, the basic principals are the same and I have kept things simple so as not to confuse you with too much data.

TABLE 17.3

	2013 £m	2012 £m
Sales	650	700
Cost of sales (materials)	300	340
Gross profit	350 (54%)	360 (51%)
Expenses	100	120
Profit before interest and taxation	250	240
Interest	30	40
Profit before taxation	220	200
Taxation	66	60
Profit after taxation	154	140
Dividends paid to shareholders	40	50
Profit retained	114	90

Note: Gross profit is sometimes referred to as gross margin. It is also often expressed as a percentage of sales and called the gross profit percentage or gross margin percentage. In our example for 2013 it is 54% (350 as a percentage of 650).

TABLE 17.4

	2013 £m	2012 £m
Fixed assets:		
Plant and equipment (after depreciation)	150	160
Current assets:		
Stock	200	250
Debtors	150	170
Cash at bank	50	60
Current liabilities:		
Trade creditors	(160)	(180)
Bank overdraft	(100)	(110)
Net current assets:	140	190
Total fixed and net current assets:	**290**	**350**
Capital and reserves:		
Called up share capital	150	150
Retained profits	140	26
Term loan	–	174
	290	**350**

Note that the company has been able to repay the term loan of £174m during the year by retaining profits of £114m and reducing total fixed and net current assets by £60m.

We will now use these accounts to undertake ratio analysis and compare the results of 2013 against 2012 in order to get a better understanding of how the company has performed. Shareholders, future investors, lenders and other stakeholders will use published accounts and ratio analysis to help make their decisions. Of course, the information in year-end accounts is largely out of date and they will also refer to interim accounts, management accounts and other information.

Ratio analysis

As we have discussed in previous chapters executives need up-to-date performance indicators. Ratio analysis is a way of gaining a better understanding of financial performance. They enable comparisons between periods and with other companies. They enable us to track efficiency and profitability. They can be used to reveal trends in profitability, efficiency, gearing, liquidity and returns on investment. We will restrict this chapter to explaining some of the more commonly used and, therefore, useful financial ratios.

Gross profit percentage

This ratio is sometimes called the gross margin. It is probably the most widely used and quoted ratio. It shows the ratio of gross profit to sales expressed as a percentage.

In our example above for the year 2013 the gross profit was £350m and sales were £650m.

The gross profit percentage is:

$$\frac{\text{Gross profit}}{\text{Sales}} \times \frac{100}{1}$$

$$\frac{£350m}{£650} \times \frac{100}{1}$$

Gross profit percentage = **54%**

This is an improvement on the previous year when the gross profit percentage was 51%. An analyst would compare these gross profit percentages with those achieved in similar businesses.

The gross profit percentage can also be used as a useful measure to compare the contribution that individual product sales make towards a company's overall fixed costs.

Net profit percentage

This ratio compares net profit to sales and is calculated as follows:

$$\frac{\text{Net profit}}{\text{Sales}} \times \frac{100}{1}$$

In the above example for X Ltd the net profit (after tax and interest) ratio for 2013 is:

$$\frac{£154}{£650} \times \frac{100}{1}$$

Net profit percentage = **24%**

This ratio indicates that the net profit after interest and taxation is 24% of sales.

Another net profit ratio often quoted by analysts is Net Profit Before Interest & Taxation. This will be shown as NBIT.

There are a number of variations used by analysts when quoting net profit ratios and you need to be sure that you understand what an analyst has used so that you can compare like with like.

Current ratio

This ratio measures the solvency of a business by comparing current assets with current liabilities. It is normally shown just as a single figure.

$$\text{Current ratio} = \frac{\text{Current assets}}{\text{Current liabilities}}$$

Using figures from the balance sheet of X Ltd for 2013:

Stock and work in progress	200
Debtors	150
Cash at bank	<u>50</u>
Total current assets	400
Trade creditors	(160)
Bank overdraft	<u>(100)</u>
Total current liabilities	(260)
Current ratio	$= \dfrac{400}{260}$
Current ratio	$=$ **1.54**

Since this is a positive number it indicates that on a going concern basis the company is solvent. However, the company does have to collect its debts and convert its stock into sales and ultimately cash in order to be able to pay its creditors. Remember also that bank overdrafts are repayable on demand. There is a stricter test of a company's actual liquidity rather than just its solvency and this is called the liquidity ratio, which is explained below.

Liquidity ratio

The liquidity ratio indicates a company's ability to repay its debts as they fall due. It is usually expressed as a single figure. A figure that is greater than '1' would indicate that the company is liquid. A ratio of less than '1' would indicate that the company might struggle to pay debts when they are due.

$$\text{Liquidity ratio} = \frac{\text{Liquid assets}}{\text{Current liabilities}}$$

Liquid assets are cash and debtors. Stock is not a liquid asset since it still has to be converted into a sale.

In our example for X Ltd the liquidity ratio for 2013 is:

$$\text{Liquidity ratio} = \frac{150 + 50}{260}$$

$$\text{Liquidity ratio} = 0.77$$

Since this liquidity ratio is less than one it might indicate that the company could have problems in repaying debts as they fall due. It will certainly need to ensure that it collects cash from its own debtors before it can pay all of its creditors. Although this company appears to be profitable it does need to ensure that it does not 'overtrade' and find itself without enough liquidity. Perhaps it needs to convert some of its stock more quickly into sales and reduce stock levels even further.

This ratio is useful in highlighting areas for management attention.

Stock turnover ratio

This ratio measures how fast stock moves through a business. Holding on to stock is expensive since there is an interest cost on funds invested in stock and there are also other holding costs such as warehousing and storage. Also, stock may degrade if held for too long. Conversely, it might be beneficial to buy stocks early at a time of rising prices and also to take advantage of any quantity discounts by purchasing greater quantities than are immediately needed by the production department. If stock levels are kept too low then there might be a chance of not having material required to meet production schedules or to make up customer orders. There is an optimal level of stock that needs to be held and this requires careful calculation.

The stock turnover ratio is just a simple measure of how quickly stock moves and a high stock turnover number would generally be considered healthy since fewer funds were being tied up in stock. Be aware that stock turnover ratios calculated using year-end figures can be concealing significant movements during the accounting period. In other words, the year-end value of stock may not reflect average stock values. This consideration also applies to other ratios that have been calculated using year-end values. The calculation for stock turnover usually uses average stock values.

$$\text{Stock turnover} = \frac{\text{Cost of sales (material costs only)}}{\text{Average stock values}}$$

The average stock value can be calculated in the case of X Ltd by using the opening and closing values of stock and dividing them by 2.

$$\text{Average stock} = \frac{200 + 250}{2}$$

$$\text{Average stock} = 225$$

$$\text{Stock turnover} = \frac{300 \text{ (cost of sales, materials)}}{225 \text{ (material cost)}}$$

$$\text{Stock turnover} = \textbf{1.33 times p.a.}$$

This is a slow rate of stock turnover. It may well be necessary in this type of business. However, it is not good for liquidity as indicated in the liquidity ratio previously mentioned. In means that the company will need to ensure it has sufficient funds to invest in stock and is aware of the significant stock holding cost.

Debtors' days

Debtors' days is an indication of how good a company is at collecting debts from its customers and how much trade credit it allows. The fewer days the better.

The calculation for debtor days is:

$$\text{Debtors' days} = \frac{\text{Debtors}}{\text{Sales}} \times 365$$

In the case of X Ltd for 2013:

$$\text{Debtors' days} = \frac{150}{650} \times 365$$

$$\text{Debtors' days} = \textbf{84 days}$$

Again, this would not generally be considered a good sign since 84 days is slow. Of course, it depends upon the business. For example, a car repair business may have debtor days of just five whilst an undertaker may consider 90 days to be normal.

Average balances can be used to calculate debtors' days. Also, it is often more helpful to show the value of debtors falling into different period categories such as: 0–30 days, 31–60 days, 61–90 days and over 90 days.

It can now be seen that the poor liquidity ratio of company X Ltd is mainly caused by poor debt collection and a poor stock turnover as indicated in the ratios.

Fixed assets turnover ratio

This measures the efficiency of fixed asset usage by comparing fixed assets with sales. It is calculated as follows:

$$\text{Fixed assets turnover ratio} = \frac{\text{Sales turnover}}{\text{Fixed assets}}$$

In the case of X Ltd this will be:

$$\text{Fixed assets turnover ratio} = \frac{650}{150}$$

$$\text{Fixed assets turnover ratio} = \textbf{4 times p.a.}$$

This is one ratio that varies enormously depending on the type of business. For example, a manufacturing company with heavy plant and equipment may have a greater fixed asset value than a marketing agency with a similar sales turnover. Again, it is useful to use average fixed asset values rather than end of year balances.

Gearing ratio

This important ratio shows the level of a company's external borrowing compared to its equity (shareholder's funds). A company is said to be highly geared when it has a high level of external borrowing compared to equity. One way of expressing gearing is as a simple percentage as follows:

$$\text{Gearing} = \frac{\text{External loans}}{\text{Internal equity}}$$

Assuming a company has bank loans outstanding of £700,000 and shareholders' funds (called up capital and retained earnings) of £3,500,000 then the gearing ratio will be:

$$\text{Gearing ratio} = \frac{700,000}{3,500,000}$$

Gearing ratio = **20%**

This result will generally be considered as healthy and as a lowly geared company. As with other ratios it all depends on the type of business.

In our example we have shown gearing as the ratio of loans to equity. Some analysts may show it other ways. For example, they may show gearing as the ratio of loan capital to total capital (loans + equity). When comparing gearing ratios always be sure that you are comparing ratios using the same methods/formulae. Gearing may also be calculated using market values. For the purpose of clarity I am sticking with the basic method that demonstrates the principal of gearing.

Return on capital employed ratio

The return on equity ratio is often referred to as ROCE. This ratio compares profits with the capital employed to earn the profits.

$$\text{ROCE \%} = \frac{\text{Profit before interest \& tax}}{\text{Capital employed}}$$

There are various definitions for capital employed. Often it is defined as shareholders' funds plus term loans.

If a company makes a profit before interest and tax of £250,000 when shareholders' funds were £500,000 and term loans were £100,000 then the ROCE would be:

$$\text{ROCE} = \frac{250,000}{500,000 + 100,000}$$

ROCE = 42%

This means that for every £1 of capital employed in the company there is a profit (before interest and tax) of 42p.

Return on equity

The return on equity (ROE) ratio shows the rate of return achieved by the equity investors in a company. It is expressed as the percentage of profit before interest and tax (PBIT) is to equity.

$$ROE = \frac{PBIT}{Equity}$$

In the case of X Ltd for the year ended 2013 this would be:

$$ROE = \frac{250}{290}$$

$$ROCE = \textbf{86\%}$$

Earnings per share (EPS)

This is the amount of earnings attributable to each equity share. For example, if a company has paid up capital of 100,000 ordinary shares of £5 and makes a net profit after tax of £50,000 then the earnings per share will equal 50p per share. Simply divide the net profit after tax by the number of shares.

$$Earnings\ per\ share\ (EPS) = \frac{Net\ profit\ after\ tax}{Number\ of\ ordinary\ shares}$$

$$EPS = \frac{£50,000}{100,000}$$

$$EPS = \textbf{50p per share}$$

The price earnings ratio (PER)

The purpose of this ratio is to compare the actual earnings per share with the market price of one ordinary share.

$$PER = \frac{Market\ price\ of\ ordinary\ share}{Earnings\ per\ share\ (EPS)}$$

Assuming the market price of the above shares is £6 and that the earnings per share are 50p then the price earnings ratio would be:

$$PER = \frac{£6}{50p}$$

$$PER = 12$$

The PER shows the relationship between return and market price and is, therefore, of importance to investors and the market.

Earnings yield

This is another way of expressing the price earnings ratio (PER).

$$\text{Earnings yield} = \frac{EPS}{\text{Share price}} \times \frac{100}{1}$$

Using the figures above:

$$\text{Earnings yield} = \frac{50p}{£6} \times \frac{100}{1}$$

$$\text{Earnings yield} = 8.3\%$$

Dividend cover

This shows us how many times a dividend could have been paid from earnings. It is measured as a number and the higher the number the better the cover.

$$\text{Dividend cover} = \frac{\text{Earnings per share}}{\text{Dividend per share}}$$

If a company has earnings per share of 50p and pays a dividend of 10p on each share then the dividend cover will be 5 times.

$$\text{Dividend cover} = \frac{50p}{10p}$$

$$\text{Dividend cover} = 5 \text{ times}$$

Dividend yield

The dividend yield shows the dividend return against the market value of an investment.

$$\text{Dividend yield} = \frac{\text{Dividend}}{\text{Share price}} \times \frac{100}{1}$$

If a dividend of 10p is paid when the market price of a share is £6 the dividend yield will be:

$$\text{Dividend yield} = \frac{10p}{£6} \times \frac{100}{1}$$

$$\text{Dividend yield} = \mathbf{1.7\%}$$

You can use an Excel spreadsheet as we have done in Figure 17.1 for the above analysis. Use a different sheet for each type of ratio.

You can use the templates above or online templates for establishing formulae. However, it is best to calculate your own formula and test your results using the above definitions. For example, the Excel formula for gross margin % when A1 = COGS and B1 = Sales is: = **((B1−A1)/B1)*100**. Populate a spreadsheet and see if this works. Then you can prepare formulae for the other ratios you require. Online templates can help you avoid reinventing the wheel but they rarely fit with your own specific company requirements. There are many sites where accountants and analysts have shared their templates. They can save you time but will, of course, still need testing and you might also find that the time you spend trying to make your data and requirement fit into the template takes longer than just preparing your own spreadsheet.

Summary

In this chapter we have used Excel to model a profit and loss statement, balance sheet and ratio analysis. We have also explained with an example the more important ratios that an executive will need to monitor company performance.

Ratio analysis is a useful tool. It draws attention to areas that need further examination and explanations. You will have noticed that in this chapter I have used words such as generally, usually and depending. This is because we need to take care not to jump to conclusions when using ratio analysis. It is a tool to guide our questioning and for further analysis. Don't jump in and make the wrong diagnosis!

You may also have noticed that ratios are connected to each other. Some professional analysts like to link ratios together using a method called the Du Pont system. The value of this is that given only a certain amount of information it might be possible to obtain a fuller picture by deduction. Use Excel to fill in the 'gaps'.

In this chapter we have covered the essential ratios that are used to provide a guide to business performance. At this stage you should know:

- how data is imported from the ledger trial balance;
- how to use the Excel template to prepare a P&L and balance sheet;
- how to use Excel to calculate ratios;
- the basic layout of a P&L account and balance sheet;
- how to analyse accounts and ask pertinent questions using ratio analysis as a base;
- how to prepare your own Excel formulae.

Ratio analysis can become addictive in that once you have become proficient you might find yourself comparing and analysing accounts whenever they are published. This is good practice and will enable you to make comparisons between companies and seek answers. For example, if you notice two companies selling the same product that have very different gross margins ask why this should be. Is there a difference in scale of operations? Do the companies operate in different markets? Is there a difference in the quality of what appear to be similar products? Is one company more efficient than the other? Is there a difference in brand strength? This type of approach will enable you to gain a better understanding of the industry sector and help you make better executive decisions.

Finally, online templates might not save you time and will need testing. It might be quicker to simply prepare your own spreadsheets for the more basic ratio and financial analysis.

CHAPTER EIGHTEEN

FINANCIAL FUNCTIONS

We have discussed net present value and the importance of the effect of time on the value of money when undertaking investment appraisals. Excel provides some useful financial functions that will enable you to undertake business and financial modelling.

Below are some basic financial formulae that you can use directly or code into Excel. I have also summarized some of the Excel financial functions that I think you are most likely to use.

Financial formulae and using Excel *fx* functions

Basic compound interest

$$P(1 + i)^n$$
£10 @ 10% p.a. for 2 years
$$£10(1.1)^2$$
$$= £12.10$$

Using the Excel 'fx' function

$$(1 + i)^n = POWER(B3,B4)$$

Where:

Cell value

P = B1	10
i = B2	0.1
1 + B2 = B3	1.1
n = B4	1.21
FV = B1*B5	£12.10

FIGURE 18.1 Excel compound interest spreadsheet

	A	B	C
1	P	£10	
2	i	0.1	
3	1+i	1.1	
4	n	2	
5	1+iPWRn	1.21	
6	**FV**	**£12.10**	
7			

You will notice that several of the cells in Figure 18.1 have markers in their top right-hand corners. This is because I have made reference comments on these cells as a way of documenting what they contain. This will be of use for future users. Simply hover over the cell and the comment will appear. To add a comment in Excel use the following procedure:

- Select the cell that you want to add a comment to.
- Go to REVIEW and under COMMENTS select NEW COMMENT.
- Type in your comment and then click in another cell.

The comment can now be read by any user who hovers over the cell. This can help protect the model from misuse.

Frequent compounding

$$P\left(1 + \frac{i}{m}\right)^{mn}$$

£8 for 3 months @ 20% p.a. credited monthly will be:

$$£8\left(1 + \frac{0.2}{12}\right)^{3 \times 1}$$

$$= £8.41$$

Effective rate

$$\left(1 + \frac{i}{m}\right)^{m} - 1$$

1 ½ % per month on outstanding balance

$$\left(1 + \frac{0.015}{1}\right)^{12} - 1$$

$$= 19.56\%$$

Annuity

$$P\left(\frac{(1 + i)^{n} - 1}{i}\right)$$

£50 p.a. for each of 3 years at 10% p.a.

$$50\left(\frac{(1 + 0.1)^{3} - 1}{0.1}\right)$$

$$50(3.31)$$

$$= £165.50$$

Sinking fund

$$\frac{P}{\left(\dfrac{(1 + i)^{n} - 1}{i}\right)}$$

How much is required to produce £165.50 in 3 years' time when interest is 10% p.a.?

$$\frac{£165.50}{3.31}$$

$$= £50$$

Present value

$$\frac{I}{(I + i)^n}$$

This is the formula used to derive the discount tables in the Appendix. What is the present value of £165.50 to be received in 3 years' time when inflation is 10% p.a.?

$$£165.50 \times \frac{I}{(I + 0.1)^3}$$

$$= £124.34$$

Present value of annuity

$$P \times \frac{I - \dfrac{I}{(I + i)^n}}{i}$$

What is the present value of £50 p.a. for 3 years @ 10%?

$$£50 \times \frac{I - \dfrac{I}{(I.I)^3}}{0.I}$$

$$= £124.34$$

Excel financial functions

In the basic compound interest formula above I have shown an Excel formula that can calculate the future value of a principal sum with compound interest for any number of years. You can populate your own spreadsheet with the above formulae data to derive your own Excel code lines.

Excel has a number of useful ready-made financial functions that will save you time and possible errors. They can be found under '*fx*'. Some of the more common codes are:

Principal amount

CUMPRINC (rate,nper,pv,start_period,end_period,type)
Returns the cumulative principal paid on a loan between two periods.

Future value

FV (rate,nper,pmt,pv,type)
Returns the future value of an investment based on a periodic, constant payments and a constant interest rate.

FVSCHEDULE (principal,schedule)
Returns the future value of an initial principal after applying a series of compound interest rates.

Interest

IPMT (rate,per,nper,pv,fv,type)
Returns the interest payment for a given period for an investment, based on periodic, constant payments and a constant interest rate.

ISPMT (rate,per,nper,pv)
Returns the interest paid during a specific period of an investment.

NOMINAL (effect_rate,npery)
Returns the annual nominal interest rate.

Internal rate of return (IRR)

IRR (values,guess)
Returns the internal rate of return for a series of cash flows where 'guess' is the number that you guess to be close to the expected IRR.

Net present value (NPV)

NPV (rate,value1, value2,...)
Returns the net present value of an investment based on a discount rate and a series of future payments (negative values) and income (positive values)

Payment

PMT (rate,nper,pv,fv,type)
Calculates the payment for a loan based on constant payments and a constant interest rate.

Present value

PV (rate,nper,pmt,fv,type)
Returns the present value on an investment: the total amount that a series of future payments is worth now.

Summary

In this short chapter I have described the financial formulae that you might require in financial models and in particular investment appraisal. I have shown the actual formulae which are derived from $(1 + i)^n$ and how these are applied to answer certain financial questions. I have shown how to code formulae onto an Excel spreadsheet and prepare a template to use with different values. I have also listed some of the more commonly used Excel *fx* functions. There are many more financial functions available on Excel that you can use if appropriate to your business.

CHAPTER NINETEEN

BUILDING A BUSINESS MODEL

So far in this book we have described many of the different techniques and methods used in business and financial modelling. In this chapter we will use some of these to build a model for a small start-up business.

Modelling a start-up business

For the purpose of this example we will consider two brothers who are considering setting up a garden design and landscape business. They have previous experience as employees in this type of work and some understanding of the market. However, they have no experience of developing, running and maintaining a business and have asked you to advise and to help them build a business model.

Start with a template

As a first step you will need information. This will be necessary to decide if the business is viable and to build a working model. Do this by getting the brothers to complete, with your help, the following template:

FIGURE 19.1 Business start-up template

What are our assets and resources?	What are we good at and enjoy doing?	What do prospective customers really need?	What is our value proposition and how can we develop this?
Where are the customers?	How do we reach customers?	What are the channels to market? How do we find and reach customers?	Who are our key partners?
What are our key activities?	How will we manage customer relationships?	How will we segment our customers?	Who are our competitors? What is their proposition?
What is our unique selling proposition?	What are our strengths, weaknesses, opportunities and threats?	What type of organization (sole trader, partnership, limited company) and what are the taxation considerations?	What are the market prices? What are our costs and margins?
How will we be funded, equity/loan/gearing?		What return is required by investors/lenders?	
What are the risks? Do the expected returns reward the risks adequately?			
How will we meet regulatory, legal, environmental, ethical and professional standards?			

Before we can start to answer financial investment and return questions we will need to understand the viability of the business based upon known fact and reliable research.

The brothers will know the assets and skills they have and may also have some understanding of customer needs. However, they will need to scan the market and the competitive environment in order to answer most of the questions in the template.

Using the above template has produced the following results:

FIGURE 19.2   Completed business start-up template

What are our assets and resources?	What are we good at and enjoy doing?	What do prospective customers really need?	What is our value proposition and how can we develop this?
Health, horticultural training, design school degree, service knowledge, customer management experience, £30,000 cash, van/trailer (£5,000), equipment, chainsaw and H&S certificates, national award for a garden design	Designing, building and maintaining gardens. Three services could be: Design Build Maintain	Gardens to enjoy that increase the value of their property	Valuable new gardens from initial concept through to full implementation and maintenance – one stop (with key partners)

What additional assets do we need?	Where are the customers?	How do we reach customers? What are the channels to market? How do we find and reach customers?	Who are our key partners?
Digger, dumper, staff, storage space	S.E England and beyond for larger projects	Mail drop, advertorial, through partners, referrals, all supported through website. 30 drops to get a meeting	Builders, service technicians, introducers

What are our key activities? What will overheads cost?	How will we manage customer relationships?	How will we segment our customers?	Who are our competitors? What is their proposition?
1) Designing 2) Illustration to support design 3) Project planning & management 4) Customer relationships 5) Marketing and sales 6) Landscaping 7) Planting 8) Maintenance 9) Managing partnerships 10) Business management & finance Overheads: £30K p.a.	By setting customer expectations, agreeing these, meeting the expectations, regular customer reviews. Invoicing to be on agreed project stage completion events	Geography Ability to pay Size of garden Private sector Public sector Budget Average contract to be £75,000	1) Regional landscape contractors 2) Small one-man niche providers 3) Celebrity gardeners with key partnerships 4) DIY gardeners 5) Indirect competitors since gardens are a discretionary spend

FIGURE 19.2 *continued*

What is our unique selling proposition?	What are our strengths, weaknesses, opportunities and threats?	What type of organization (sole trader, partnership, limited company) and what are the taxation considerations?	What are the market prices? What are our costs and margins?
We help customers visualize a plan with an artist's illustration. Our partners have won awards	*Strengths:* Skill, energy, USP *Weaknesses:* Health – no back-up *Opportunities:* Low interest rates create a desire to spend rather than invest. *Threats:* Deep recession, competitive low-cost providers	Limited private company with VAT registration and paying small company corporation tax rates. Limited liability for shareholders. Public liability, PII insurance, employer's and other insurances	*Prices:* Labour £10–£15 p.h. Design: £35 p.h. Planning: £30 p.h. Project mgt: £30 p.h. Van/trailer: £0.60 p.m. Digger: £150 p.d. Dumper: £120 p.d Materials/plants: Quote Direct labour = 70% of direct costs *Costs:* Depreciation Staff Marketing Fuel Storage hire Insurances *Gross margins:* Approximately 50%

How will we be funded, equity/loan/gearing?	What return is required by investors/lenders?
£30,000 equity £30,000 bank overdraft for debtors Lease or L/T loan for equipment/plant	Equity 20% p.a. and proprietors salaries of £40K p.a. each Overdraft: 9% p.a. Lease: 12% p.a.

What are the risks? How will you cover these risks? Do the expected returns reward the risks adequately?
The greatest risks are: health of a key proprietor, staff or customer claims, slow payers, no customers, cash flow problems.
These risks will be covered by insurance, limited liability and through good working capital management.
The expected returns reward the identified risks

How will we meet regulatory, legal, environmental, ethical and professional standards?
Through advice from the Regional Business & Enterprise Group. One of the proprietors to be responsible for ensuring compliance and audit

The area shaded grey shows the funding required, what investors want from the business and what rate of interest lenders will require. This template collects the information that will help identify whether the risks to be undertaken will produce the required returns and will also show how business will be undertaken. It also forms a basis for the preparation of a business plan, which we will discuss later in this chapter.

The template information is useful input data and, therefore, a good place from which we can start to build our model.

Opening balance sheet

We will start with an expected opening balance sheet assuming that a long-term loan has been arranged with a first charge over plant and equipment and a floating charge over all other assets.

Balance sheet at 1/1/2013

	£ Sterling
Fixed assets:	
Plant & equipment	70,000
Van/trailer	5,000
Current assets:	
Cash in bank	60,000
Total assets:	**135,000**
Ordinary share capital	35,000
Bank overdraft	30,000
Term loan (secured)	70,000
Total liabilities	**135,000**

This is how the company will look before any business has been transacted.

Expected returns for risk – proprietors' pay, bank interest

The next step is to determine what the investor/proprietors and lenders require from the business in the first 12 months. If we start by determining what we want out of the business we can, later on, calculate what we need to put in to achieve this return. This is, therefore, a bottom-up approach. We can, of course, start our model at various stages depending upon the information that is available; in this case we know what the brothers and bankers expect as a return for the risks they are undertaking and it computes to £98,100 (say £100K) as indicated below.

TABLE 19.1

Investors:	Return of shares	£35,000 @ 20% p.a.	£7,000
	Salaries	£40,000 × 2	£80,000
Lenders:	Overdraft	£30,000 @ 9% p.a.	£2,700
	Term loan	£70,000 @ 12% p.a.	£8,400
Total requirement			£98,100
			(say £100K)

Assuming that the rate of tax is 25%, this indicates that the business must produce a minimum profit before interest and tax as follows:

Profit before salaries, interest and taxation	£100,433
Proprietors' salaries	£80,000
Profit before interest and taxation	£20,433
Interest	£11,100
Profit after interest	£9,333
Taxation at 25%	£2,333
Profit after tax	£7,000
Dividend	£7,000
Retained profit	£0

This means that the company must make a profit before investors' salaries, interest and taxation of around £100K in order to meet the return required by the risk takers. You can arrive at this conclusion by starting with the bottom figure and working back up the table using figures and information collected in the start-up template.

Forecast profit and loss statement and sales requirement

Having established that we need a minimum of £100K of profit before tax we can now determine the sales and margins required. Using the figures from the start-up template the forecast P&L and sales requirements can be calculated from the bottom up as follows:

	£000s
Sales	290
Gross margin (50%)	145
Overheads	30
Depreciation £75K @ 20%	15
Profit before interest, taxation and salaries	100

(We know what profit is required to provide a return to shareholders, pay salaries and pay the bank's interest. We also know what the depreciation and overheads are and the gross margin percentage. We can, therefore, calculate the level of sales required).

To provide the required return to the risk takers we will need sales of: £290,000 p.a.

Required marketing and selling activity

To win £290,000 of sales we will need a certain level of marketing and sales activity. The brothers felt that their previous experience has indicated that the most effective way of winning new business is through a targeted mail drop followed up by a consultation meeting.

The level of sales and marketing activity is calculated as follows:

Sales required	£290,000
Average contract size required	£75,000
Number of contracts needed £290,000/£75,000	4 p.a.
Number of sales meeting to close one contract	3
Number of sales meeting needed 4 × 3	12
Number of targeted leaflet drops to get a meeting	30
Number of targeted leaflet drops required 30 × 12	360

The company will need to drop 360 leaflets and have 12 sales meetings to win the sales required. This is a very low level of activity compared to other businesses and is due to local knowledge and precision targeting – not a scatter approach.

Direct costs required

The direct labour and material required will be Sales less Gross Margin:

$$£290K - £145K = £145K$$

70% of direct cost is labour.
The average direct labour cost per hour is $(£10+£15)/2 = £12.50$
The direct labour hours are: $(£145K \times 70\%)/£12.50 = 8,120$ hours p.a.

Building a model

Having worked out a base case for the levels of activity required, sales, costs and margins we can now begin to prepare a model that will help us focus each week on what needs to be done to ensure we reach our objective of rewarding the risk takers. We can use Excel for this and an example is given in Figure 19.3.

We have considered just three cases.

Base case – using above figures derived from the business start-up template.
Case 1 – assuming a 21% increase in sales.
Case 2 – assuming a 21% reduction in sales.
Case 3 – assuming that initial equity is reduced by £20K and replaced by a term loan.

An example of the coding is column 'F':

Equity = F9 – F4 – F5 – F7 – F8
Direct costs = –F11*0.5
Gross margin = SUM(F11:F12)
PBIT&S = SUM(F13:F15)
Interest = (F7*0.09) + (F8*0.12)
Taxation = –(F16 + F17 + F18)*0.25
Profit after tax = SUM(F16:F9)
Retained = SUM(F20:F21)
Sales drops = F11*1.241
Direct labour = –(F12*0.7)/26
Gearing ratio = F6/(F7 + F8)
Profit as % of sales = F20/F11

Sensitivities:

Case 1 – a 21% increase in sales = 314% increase in profit after tax.

Case 3 – increasing gearing = increased interest cost = reduced profit but greater return on shareholders' investment. By reducing the shareholders' investment from £35K to £15K their return has increased from 20% to 33%.

FIGURE 19.3 Business model

	A	B	C	D	E	F	G
1	**Business model**						
2	**£000s**		Base case	Case 1	Case 2	Case 3	
3			01/01/2013	01/01/2013	01/01/2013	01/01/2013	
4	Fixed assets		75	75	75	75	
5	Current assets		60	60	60	60	
6	Equity		-35	-35	-35	-15	
7	Overdraft		-30	-30	-30	-30	
8	Term loan		-70	-70	-70	-90	
9	Total		0	0	0	0	
10			1/13–12/13	1/13–12/13	1/13–12/13	1/13–12/13	
11	Sales		290	350	230	290	
12	Direct costs		-145	-175	-115	-145	
13	Gross margin		145	175	115	145	
14	Overheads		-30	-30	-30	-30	
15	Depreciation		-15	-15	-15	-15	
16	PBIT&S		100	130	70	100	
17	Interest		-11	-11	-11	-14	
18	Prop. salaries		-80	-80	-80	-80	
19	Tax		-2	-10	5	-2	
20	Profit after tax		7	29	-16	5	
21	Dividend		-7	-7	-7	-7	
22	Retained		0	22	-23	-2	
23							
24	Sales drops		360	434	285	360	
25	Direct labour hours		8120	9800	6440	8120	
26	Average labour rate		0.0125	0.0125	0.0125	0.0125	
27	Gearing ratio		35%	35%	35%	13%	
28	Profit less tax/sales		2%	8%	-7%	2%	
29	Return on equity		20%	82%	-45%	33%	
30	Base case assumes sales of £290 p.a, Case 1 = sales + 21%, Case 2 = sales – 21%						
31	Case 3 assumes reduced equity replaced by term loan						
32	Outputs shown in grey shade						
33							

This simple model can be extended to include many scenarios and cases. The purpose of a model is to show:

key activities;

how these translate into results.

An early activity of this start-up company will be to design, print and drop 360 targeted sales leaflets, receive calls and follow up with sales meetings. It will also need to have labour and resources (equipment and funds) available. The Excel model will be the basis for management reporting and a dashboard of key indicators to continually measure performance.

Key indicators

For this particular start-up company the initial key indicators are:

- number of leaflet drops;
- number of sales meetings;
- number of conversions;
- direct labour hours available;
- sales;
- gross margins;
- net profit %;
- return on equity;
- gearing ratio.

Excel dashboard software is available to produce high-quality visual dashboards suitable for board meetings. You can view some examples by searching on Google for 'Excel Dashboards'. As an alternative you can simply use the chart facility on Excel to produce line or other style charts for the KPIs you have selected. An example is given in Figure 19.4.

FIGURE 19.4 Example of KPI chart

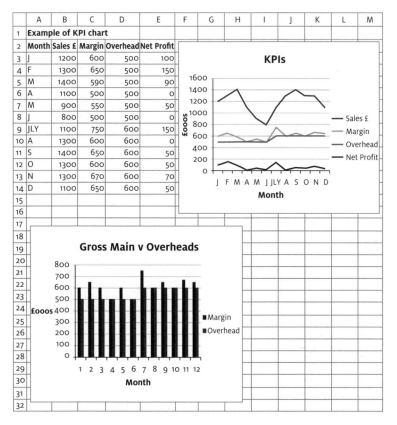

	A	B	C	D	E	F	G	H	I	J	K	L	M
1	Example of KPI chart												
2	Month	Sales £	Margin	Overhead	Net Profit								
3	J	1200	600	500	100								
4	F	1300	650	500	150								
5	M	1400	590	500	90								
6	A	1100	500	500	0								
7	M	900	550	500	50								
8	J	800	500	500	0								
9	JLY	1100	750	600	150								
10	A	1300	600	600	0								
11	S	1400	650	600	50								
12	O	1300	600	600	50								
13	N	1300	670	600	70								
14	D	1100	650	600	50								

The initial approach used by the brothers will be to simply review their key activities on a weekly basis.

For example:

TABLE 19.2

Key activities in week one	Result	Next step
Day 1 180 leaflet drops	Received 9 phone call enquiries	Arrange 2 meetings
Days 2 & 3 Receive calls Attend 2 meetings	Attended 2 meetings & obtained 1 request for proposal	Prepare outline plan/proposal and present to prospect
Day 4 Prepare outline proposal	Outline proposal and cost estimates drafted	Present to customer
Day 5 Present proposal to prospect Seek prospect agreement to pay for full plan	Interest and request for plan and initial drawings	Prepare contract
Day 6 Prepare contract	Contract e-mailed to prospect	Await response and discuss

Activity in the first week will be sales. If they are successful in obtaining a signed contract then the activities in the following week will be arranging resources (labour, materials, equipment) and ordering plants. Sales and marketing activity must also be maintained. This will require handling further calls from the initial leaflet drop, attending prospect meetings and considering when to drop the remainder of the leaflets. For a small start-up landscape business managing sales activity with site work can be a challenge. New business needs to be secured before current business is completed.

Business plan

The information collected from the business start-up template can also be used to prepare a formal business plan. This is a document used to help guide the executive team and to advise investors and lenders.

A business plan for the garden design business will include the following:

Overview

To create outstanding garden designs that will increase the enjoyment and value of a property. Services will include design, illustration, detailed planting, irrigation and maintenance. The target market is properties in the South East of England with a market value of £2m upwards. Garden projects will be £75K upwards, producing gross margins of 50%.

The executive team are experienced in this market and comprise: (names and CVs attached).

Initial funding will be provided by the executive team. Additional working capital by way of a bank overdraft will be secured over plant and equipment. One of the initial risks with this start-up is the development of new business. The team have an initial project through existing relationships that will serve as a reference and they have a workable sales plan.

The market

According to Land Registry data analysed by Lloyds Bank 1,518 homes valued at more than £2 million were sold in the UK in 2011 – a rise of 5% on 2010. The executive team estimate that the majority of these were in the South East of England. When a property changes hands there is often an opportunity to build a new garden for the new owners and the team will target these with their leaflets. Change of ownership is obtained through a variety of online sources including council sites.

Unique selling proposition

Illustrations to support initial plans. These show how the garden will look in one to five years' time.

Hampton Court award-winning team.

One-stop services from initial consultations through to full implementation and maintenance.

Channels to market

References and existing contacts, targeted leaflet drops, website search engine utilization, Hampton Court exhibition.

Competition

There are few direct one-shop competitors. Direct competition in this market will come from connected garden designers who use contracted implementers. Lack of controlled resources is a weakness in competitors' offerings and is our own USP. There is also competition from garden landscape and maintenance companies. Gardens are a discretionary spend and there is indirect competition from all other home improvement providers. New entrants to the market may also develop our offering but will need to acquire the combined illustration, design and planning skills. There is no hard barrier to new entrants.

Risks and cover

Identified risks are:

1 Lack of new business. This is covered by the sales plan but is the most unpredictable of risks.
2 Insured risks including public liability, health and safety, employee liability and executive team health.
3 Other business management and working capital risks managed by a competent financial director.
4 Competitive risks managed through the maintenance of our USP. There are no significant barriers to new entrants.
5 Increased regulation could be a risk if not all competitors follow the rules.

The business has limited liability and an exit strategy.

Executive team, staff and training

The executive team is comprised of three directors covering business development/consultant, designer/project manager and a commercial manager/company secretary. CVs of the executive team are attached. There are three full-time employed staff plus additional contractors as required. Staff training is provided in chainsaw operation, digger/dumper driving, four-wheel drive and trailer towing, health and safety and other relevant skills.

Financials

An opening balance sheet together with estimated annual profit and cash flow projections is provided. There are targets for sales, gross margins, ROCE and other key ratios. Management reports are prepared monthly.

Economic environment

Potential clients who are not dependent on earnings but live off their investments may see a drop in their income in a period of low interest rates. However, this does not necessarily translate into a lower spend on their gardens since they may prefer to spend on a new project rather than have cash earning little interest in their bank. Clients who are dependent on earned income are vulnerable to periods of high unemployment and lay off. There is no direct correlation between the state of the economy and new business development within reasonable boundaries and the business is thought to be more robust than many.

Sensitivity analysis

A sensitivity analysis has been undertaken in the business model. The principal sensitivity is sales value. The sensitivity to all other variables can be seen in the model.

Plant and equipment

Key items of owned plant include a digger, dumper, trailer and four-wheel drive. Other specialist items such as root grinders are hired as required.

Health and safety

All staff are trained in the equipment used and comply with a site health and safety policy. A health and safety consultant is hired to advise and supervise larger projects and this is built into the pricing.

Project management

All projects are controlled using critical path analysis showing activities, milestones, dependencies and events to completion. An executive team member controls projects and invoices customers when agreed milestones are reached.

When presenting a business plan to a potential lender it is best to keep things as simple as possible but, nevertheless, to have all answers at hand. A lender will be asking the following questions:

- How competent are the management team?
- What 'skin' do they have in the business?
- How viable are their proposals?
- Is it an up and running business or should they be looking for a venture capitalist?
- How can I check cash flow and profits?
- How good is the security?
- What are the risks?
- Is the return worth the risks?
- What is the exit strategy?
- Is there the potential for future business opportunities?

Summary

Start modelling a new business by using a template to determine what you can put into and get out of the business. Identify what customers actually want. Compare and consider all competitive offerings to your own USP, your channels and market segmentation. Consider your assets, resources, gearing and how you will be funded. In this process you will identify your key activities and key performance indicators. Your model should identify these and how they will be influenced by changes in any variable input and it will help identify those key performance indicators that you need to run the business. In this case we have chosen a garden design business. This is a discretional spend so in addition to direct competition (other garden design firms) there will be indirect competition for the homeowner's spend. Consider how this can be countered and recognized in the model. If preparing a business plan for a lender consider what is important to the lender and be sure you address this.

CHAPTER TWENTY

MODELLING PROJECTS

In this chapter we will discuss the principals behind project models. Whether your project is for the construction of a North Sea oil platform or just an IT installation there are certain principals that are common to both. There are, of course, many project management applications available online and you can design your own using Excel. There are also free Microsoft Excel templates available online. However, it is worthwhile understanding the principals of project management before using any templates.

What is a project?

A project is a scheme to achieve a defined objective within a certain time. This is different from the repetitive business operations of a company. The management of a project requires different processes from managing the day-to-day operations of a business. The objective of project management is to achieve the project goals subject to the financial, resource, regulatory, time and other defined constraints. This chapter will explain how to build a project model that will enable better project management.

Projects have final objectives, activities and events along the way. Each activity will use resource and consume time (duration). One method used to show how this all comes together is called 'Critical Path Analysis'. Understanding this will enable you to model projects and make better use of project management applications.

Critical path analysis (CPA)

The critical path method was developed in the 1950s by Morgan R Walker of DuPont and James E Kelley, Jr of Remington Rand. The term 'critical path' is credited to the developers of the PERT (Program Evaluation and Review Technique): Booz Allen Hamilton and the US Navy. The critical path method is used with most large projects including oil platform construction projects, civil engineering, aerospace, defence, IT and other large constructions.

The technique of critical path analysis requires the construction of a model that includes the following:

- a list of all activities;
- the duration or time taken to complete each activity;
- the dependencies between the activities;
- events during the project;
- final objective.

Using this information a critical path analysis model shows the longest path of activities to completion and the earliest and latest times that activities can start and finish without extending the overall time to project completion.

The model will show which activities are 'critical' and which have 'float' and can be delayed without making the project longer.

This is key information especially during contract negotiations because an informed contractor will know points of weakness in a project network. Activities on the critical path cannot be delayed without extending the whole project duration and cost.

The critical path comprises the project activities that make up the longest overall duration. A delayed activity on the critical path directly extends the planned project completion date because there is no float at all on the critical path.

CPA example

Assume that a project starts at zero and has six events (the sixth event being the final objective). The duration (in days) of the activities between events is given below:

Activity (between events)	Duration (days)
0–1	1
0–2	2
1–3	3
1–4	2
2–4	2
3–4	4
3–5	2
4–5	3
5–6	1

If we now draw the above activities and events on a chart we can see the network and dependencies. See Figure 20.1.

FIGURE 20.1 Critical path analysis

Critical path = double arrow

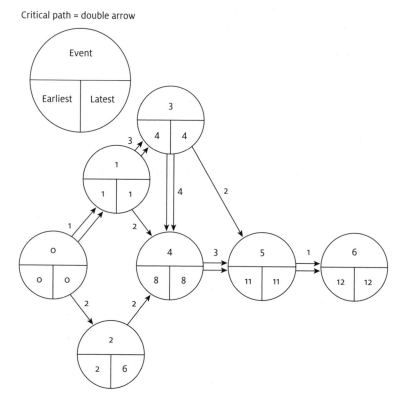

In Figure 20.1 events have been numbered 0, 1, 2, 3, 4, 5, 6.

The earliest event times are calculated by adding the activity duration on the network that gives the highest value. For example the earliest event time for event number 6 is (1+3+4 = 8) – taking the route 0–1–3–4.

The latest event time working back from 12 (in event 6) is calculated by taking the lowest value working back down through the network. For example, the latest event time for event number 3 is (12–1–3–4 = 4) – taking the route 6–5–4–3.

The critical path has been shown with double arrows. Note that the events that these double arrows join have earliest and latest times that are equal. There is no slack (float) here.

Total float

The total float of an activity is the total flexibility within which an activity can be carried out without affecting the overall time for the project. This is sometimes called the 'slack'.

Free float

The free float is the flexibility allowed for an activity if all other activities start at their earliest start times.

TABLE 20.1

Activity	Duration	E. Start	E. End	L. End	L. Start	T F	F F
0–1	1	0	1	1	0	0	0
0–2	2	0	2	6	0	4	0
1–3	3	1	4	4	1	0	0
1–4	2	1	8	8	1	5	5
2–4	2	2	8	8	6	4	4
3–4	4	4	8	8	4	0	0
3–5	2	4	11	11	4	5	5
4–5	3	8	11	11	8	0	0
5–6	1	11	12	12	11	0	0

Activity = activity between events which are number 0 to 6
Duration = time to complete each activity
E. Start = Earliest start
E. End = Earliest end
L. End = Latest end
L. Start = Latest start
TF = Total float (slack)
FF = Free float
Total float = (L. End) − (E. Start) − Activity Time (duration)
Free float = (E. End) − (E. Start) − Activity Time (duration)

Having identified the critical activities it is now possible to see if any delay in an activity will extend the overall project completion time and cost.

Each activity will have a cost attached. This could be material, labour and overhead. It could be contractors' fees.

It is possible that an activity has multiple associated contracts. This is when things start to get complicated from both a reconciliation point and also from a negotiating position. A relatively small contract may lie on a critical activity and the whole project could be vulnerable to a delay in this minor project! This is where CPA has real value in that it exposes these weaknesses and enables the project management team to identify risks and take the necessary avoiding actions.

Risk and uncertainty

Normally a project is undertaken because there is an expectation of a favourable outcome. There is a business opportunity that is expected to produce a return. However, in the way of achieving this favourable outcome are risks and uncertainties.

A risk is a possible unfavourable outcome. The chances of a risk actually happening are measured in terms of its probability. For example, there may be a 1% chance of fire or a 10% chance of a bad debt. Risks can be identified, measured and brought into the business model.

Uncertainty means that there is no certain way of identifying either a risk or measuring its probability. For this reason uncertainty is what causes dread and fear of investment. You might have heard of 'FUD'! This is a technique used by salesmen whereby Fear Uncertainty and Dread (FUD) are introduced into a selling process to encourage the potential buyer to look for a solution, which, of course, the salesperson has to offer.

Identified risks can be evaluated and brought into a business model. If there is a high level of uncertainty an investor may find it hard to make a decision or may only take an opportunity where the uncertain outcome can be spread over a larger portfolio of investments. So, if you don't know what might happen but still want to invest make sure that the potential total loss is manageable within a greater portfolio of investment opportunities.

Risk can be managed to an extent within a project. Uncertainty is best covered through a larger portfolio of projects with expected favourable outcomes and less uncertainty. Uncertainty should, in my opinion, be managed differently from risk.

Gantt charts and resource planning

Figure 20.2 is a chart based on the Gantt principal and shows the activities and their effect of resource planning. The histogram at the bottom of the chart shows the work days required. This can be particularly useful when considering human resource availability or other resource constraints. For example, in Figure 20.2 the work days required reach three. If only two work days were available then the activities would need to be rescheduled to accommodate this.

The following Gantt chart assumes that all activities start at the earliest possible time.

FIGURE 20.2 Gantt chart

Activity\Days	1	2	3	4	5	6	7	8	9	10	11	12
0–1	A											
0–2	A	A	F	F	F	F						
1–3		A	A	A								
1–4		A	A	F	F	F	F	F				
2–4			A	A	F	F	F	F				
3–4					A	A	A	A				
3–5					A	A	F	F	F	F	F	
4–5									A	A	A	
5–6												A
Work days required												
4												
3												
2												
1												

Modelling projects using Excel

There are many useful online project planning templates available to Excel users and these can be found through a Google search for project management templates. There are also online project management applications, some are free and others are available for a fee that might also be supported with training packages.

I have used the above example to prepare an Excel spreadsheet for the calculation of total and free float; details are given in Figure 20.3.

FIGURE 20.3 Calculation of total float and free float

	A	B	C	D	E	F	G	H	I
1	Calculation of total float and free float								
2									
3	Activity	Duration	E. Start	E. End	L. End	L. Start	TF	FF	
4	0–1	1	0	1	1	0	0	0	
5	0–2	2	0	2	6	0	4	0	
6	1–3	3	1	4	4	1	0	0	
7	1–4	2	1	8	8	1	5	5	
8	2–4	2	2	8	8	6	4	4	
9	3–4	4	4	8	8	4	0	0	
10	3–5	2	4	11	11	4	5	5	
11	4–5	3	8	11	11	8	0	0	
12	5–6	1	11	12	12	11	0	0	
13							18	14	
14	Key:	E. Start = Earliest Start							
15		E. End = Earliest End							
16		L. End = Latest End							
17		L. Start = Latest Start							
18		TF = Total Float							
19		FF = Free Float							
20	Formula:	TF = (L. End) – (E. Start) – Duration			For example:=E11–C11–B11				
21		FF = (E. End) – (E. Start) – Duration			For example:=D11–C11–B11				
22									
23									

Summary

In this chapter we have covered the principals of modelling projects. It is essential to have an understanding of these principals before selecting and using an online project management application. I have explained critical path analysis and the use of Gantt charts to help identify project risk, prevent slippage and help with resource management. This chapter has explained the nature of a project, risk and uncertainty and how to use models to identify and manage these.

CHAPTER TWENTY-ONE

INTEGRATION, COMPLEXITY AND BUSINESS MODELS

Big companies require solutions for managing 'big data'. One advantage that a small company has over a big company is agility and a certain lack of complexity. Therefore, if you are working for a small company, be sure not to lose these advantages by building into your model unnecessary complexity and particularly levels of integration that are not needed.

The level of integration required

It is worthwhile considering the level of integration, consolidation and data transfer that you require in your business and financial model.

Generally the larger the scale and volume of data the greater are the benefits of integration.

The benefits can be:

- potentially less error due to manual intervention;
- easier scenario planning and sensitivity analysis;
- faster processing and results;
- better live collaboration with an executive team;
- a potential saving in staff time and costs once the model is set up.

The disadvantages can be:

- errors can cascade and multiply throughout the system;
- the model assumes a life of its own and assumptions/formulae may go unquestioned;
- fewer people understand the mechanics of the system.

These disadvantages can largely be overcome by ensuring that the model is set up, backed up with competent staff and tested regularly by inputting an item of data and checking to see if the output is as expected. Protecting your model's integrity and access to it is essential.

Problems of integration normally arise in smaller companies that do not have the resource to build and police an integrated model but nevertheless attempt to introduce a high level of integration without dedicated and competent staff.

One of the earlier forms of integrated business model was the fully integrated standard costing system. This elegant model integrated financial and management accounting producing management reports that enabled executives to concentrate their attention on variances from pre-set standards. It is a form of absorption costing where overheads are absorbed into production costs and also management by exception. The system worked wonderfully for large companies such as motor manufacturers and was, in the 1960s, considered the gold standard of management reporting systems.

Problems occurred when small companies attempted to adopt the system. It is a complex system whereby entries are made in the accounts at standard costs and variations between standard and actual costs are entered into variance accounts. These entries will disclose price, usage, rate, efficiency, capacity usage and volume efficiency variances. When stock is valued in a consistent way and at the lower of cost or net realizable value some of the variances from standard may relate to the stock value and certain adjusting entries are made in the accounts. Managing all of this in an organization with just one or two accounting staff can give rise to errors and short cuts with disastrous consequences.

The potential problems inherent in the integrated standard costing system also apply to any other business and financial model. Integration and sophistication are affordable in a large organization and will bring many benefits. In a small organization integration might be more trouble than it is worth. Complexity may be considered as a nuisance. Integration may reduce complexity or it might increase it.

The business modeller who uses Excel needs a good level of Excel user experience but not at the cost of finance and business knowledge. I have worked in some organizations where members controlling key areas of the business have expert Excel skills but little knowledge of the business. Their models look wonderful and few people can keep up with their pace and fully understand the scope and operation of the models. However, they can be a complete disaster. The point here is that Excel is an excellent tool for a competent business and financial modeller; however, it does not follow that a competent Excel user will always be a good business modeller!

Data and systems integration

Data integration is all about combining data that resides in different places both internally and externally. It enables data sharing and can provide users with a common unified view of data. Data sharing within an organization may be referred to as Enterprise Information Management (EII).

System integration is about bringing together subsystems and data into one system and ensuring that the subsystems function together as a single system. It is the process of linking together different computing systems and software applications. Systems integration may assist data integration.

Data integration may require a level of systems integration. A data warehouse may be used to store data extracted from various source databases or a systems designer may construct a virtual database.

More recent trends in data integration have involved providing a unified query-interface to access real-time data enabling information to be retrieved directly from original databases.

The world is becoming more and more connected and systems are becoming increasingly connected. Therefore, data integration and sharing will become increasingly available and companies that are able to engage with this will have a real advantage.

Cloud computing

As computing and software are used more as a 'utility'-type service there are new opportunities and challenges for business model data input access and data integrity.

Cloud computing is all about the delivery of computing as a service rather than as a product. Shared computing resources, software and information are provided to users over the internet or some other network. This requires trust by a user with data. Another associated shared service is software as a service (SaaS).

Typically a user will access cloud-based applications via a web browser. The software and data are stored on banks of servers at remote locations. The idea is to give users a lower cost, more reliability, more scalability, better performance and an all-round better service than they could achieve on locally based end-user servers. Presumably, if this were not the case users would not use the Cloud.

There are three basic levels of Cloud computing, Infrastructure as a Service (IaaS), Platform as a Service (PaaS) and Software as a Service (SaaS).

Access to Cloud applications may be public via the internet, community internally or externally hosted, private for a single organization, or hybrid (public, private and community).

The level of integration for input to a business model will depend upon the Cloud architecture chosen, data security and integrity considerations. Privacy, data protection, competitive advantage and unlawful communications will be just some of the concerns to be addressed.

The level to which Cloud can be engaged for business model work will depend upon the scale of an organization and concerns over loss of competitive advantage. Not surprisingly, less commercial and smaller organizations such as universities have been early adopters of the Cloud.

Summary

There are significant benefits attached to data integration for model input. These apply more to larger organizations. For smaller organizations the benefits may not outweigh the disadvantages. In either case there are dangers associated with complexity. Errors can cascade and multiply throughout the system. Data integration and sharing is becoming increasingly available and companies that are able to engage with this in a beneficial way will have a real advantage. Cloud computing has an impact on model input and the level of integration for input to a business model will depend upon the Cloud architecture chosen, data security and integrity considerations.

CHAPTER TWENTY-TWO

BUSINESS MODELS FOR THE GREEN ECONOMY

Future challenges and opportunities

We all know that to be successful in business we must meet the transitional challenges of moving further towards a green economy. How will this affect our business and financial models? Meeting the needs of climate change and emerging environmental policies may mean additional costs for some businesses whilst for others it has created new opportunities. In this chapter we will discuss some of the factors to consider in your business models. These will include:

- production processes;
- demand for greener products and offerings;
- investor expectations;
- resourcing;
- effects of climate change;
- supply chains;
- social responsibility;
- changing models.

Production processes

There will be even more pressure to improve resource efficiency and productivity and, as energy/carbon costs continue to rise, it will be necessary to adopt whole supply chain policies to enable this to happen. This will involve increased re-use of materials, carbon capture and new innovation in production design. As there is an increased use of the lower carbon sources of electricity more companies may look at ways of using electricity for production processes.

Whilst innovation in resource use has always been on the agenda with successful companies there is now more government, supplier and customer pressure to change and adapt. For example, the UK government has made a commitment to a 50% reduction in carbon by 2025. This is 4% p.a. and is a significant change that must be factored into all business models. Production process changes will require new capital investment.

Demand for greener products and services

Consumer demand is changing towards greener products and services. This demand will increase as government policies bite. For example, the demand for electric or hybrid cars will increase further as the price of petrol increases and motor manufacturers are tracking this demand in their product development. Consumers are increasingly concerned as to how far their food has travelled. Whilst these changing demands for greener products may decrease during times of recession the longer term trend has been set in education and in government policy. When building a business model looking some years ahead how will these changes in demand affect your sales forecasts?

Investor expectations

Investors increasingly expect companies to provide sustainability reporting and there is increasing global regulation for companies to do this in their annual and management reports. This is an added accountancy cost. Investors want to know that their money is being invested in environmentally sustainable projects. They are increasingly building environmental factors into their investment appraisal models.

Investor expectations will create real opportunities for some companies but challenges for others who might need to re-invest in new capital equipment and change resource practices. Keeping ahead of the game has always been a business priority!

Resourcing

The availability of resources cannot be taken for granted. For example, some businesses need an ample supply of fresh water. In drought areas this could have a direct effect or be felt through the supply chain. The demand for certain resources may increase, having an effect on your own production costs. Innovation, increased efficiency, research into alternative methods and new supplies will help mitigate resource supply threats and this may be another factor that needs to be build into medium-term business models.

Effects of climate change and other factors

There has always been climate change. Whether our existing emissions are bringing about climate change or not, few will disagree that the climate is changing along with everything else. Change of any kind affects investment decisions and is of concern to a business modeller since it brings new opportunities and challenges.

Temperature extremes have very noticeable effects. For example, trains fail to operate in cold weather; ice and snow affect air and road transport; and heat has an effect on human productivity. All of the companies I have worked for during the past 40 years have been affected by the weather but few of them have actually factored this variable into their business models. Apart from climate change, which has some level of predictability, there are other extreme factors that, although not predictable in terms of a date or time, are in fact certainties. For example, earthquakes in New Zealand and Japan are a certainty. Should you factor such events into your business model? Risk and opportunity go together! Identified risks are measurable and might be managed through insurance. Uncertainty might not be so easily managed and may require cover through a portfolio of investments.

Environmental change creates opportunities for the developers of new technologies to export their products globally. Building earthquake-resistant buildings is a valuable transferable technology. The point here is that your business model should consider all change as an opportunity and a risk.

Supply chains

Watch out for hidden embedded risks in your supply chain! Environmental change will not just affect you directly but it can come through the supply chain and have just as great an impact. Understand where your important products originate from and how they might be affected by, for example, changes in weather or resource availability. Identify new suppliers and alternative resources. Your sensitivity analysis should not just consider price but lack of availability.

Social responsibility

Most employees would prefer to work for a company that was socially responsible. Being aware and acting on this enables a company to attract and retain staff more easily. It is not just the company's policies but also its expectation of staff to act in a socially responsible manner. A very large proportion of greenhouse gasses are emitted from workplaces. A company needs to factor-in training and development to ensure that all staff play their part in protecting their environment. Staff should be encouraged to bring forward fresh ideas.

Changing models

It is clear that many companies will need to change their way of doing business and that this will have a cost. Other companies my find significant new opportunities. Business and financial models need to consider the effects of green issues in the short-, medium- and longer term. Industries that use a lot of energy or scarce resources will be well aware of increasing costs and disruption. Businesses that have high direct or indirect transportation costs will need to consider how their business models will be affected by increasing freight costs. Supplies, customer demands and costs are affected by green issues and it is possible to predict these and build them into your business model to help form alternative strategies to meet the green challenges.

Modelling green issues

I have mentioned above just a few of the green issues that you are likely to identify that will affect your business. To introduce these into your model will require some evaluation of the likely cost/benefit and an estimation of the probability and timing of when the event might occur. An example is given below:

TABLE 22.1

Event	Impact – costs $	Impact – benefits $	Probability	Timing – start
Production processes				
Carbon capture	800,000 capex		0.9	2015
Waste recycling	20,000 capex 100,000 opex	50,000 new sales	0.9	2014
Demand for greener products				
Hybrid cars and motorcycles	2,000,000 R&D 7,000,000 capex 5,000,000 opex	9,000,000 margin	0.6	2015
Investor expectations				
Increased financial reporting	30,000 accy. fee		0.9	2013
Resourcing				
Water cost	20,000 opex		0.7	2016
Effect of oil prices on all costs	90,000 opex		0.6	2013

TABLE 22.1 *continued*

Event	Impact – costs $	Impact – benefits $	Probability	Timing – start
Climate change				
Cold weather	90,000 opex		0.7	2013
Supply chain				
Resource availability	100,000 opex		0.2	2016
Social responsibility				
Staff training	40,000 opex	20,000 retention	0.6	2014

You may place your own values against the impact of events as you see them. For example, you might consider that the benefits of staff training in areas of social responsibility are greater than just a $20,000 staff-retention benefit. Other benefits might include reduced recruitment costs and possibly savings in salaries.

Having identified the costs, benefits, probabilities and timing of green events you can now build these into your business model.

Summary

In this chapter we have highlighted just some of the green issues that might affect your business model and shown how you can evaluate these for input into your model. These business opportunities and challenges are very likely events over the next decade. Each industry will have its own method of recognizing them and your own industry or trade association will, no doubt, have formed opinions. Business Link websites are often a useful place to visit to obtain specific industry or regional data.

APPENDIX 1

Excel shortcut commands

Shortcut	Command
CTRL+SHFT+(	Unhides any hidden rows within the selection.
CTRL+SHFT+)	Unhides any hidden columns within the selection.
CTRL+SHFT+&	Applies the outline border to the selected cells.
CTRL+SHFT+_	Removes the outline border from the selected cells.
CTRL+SHFT+~	Applies the General number format in Microsoft Excel.
CTRL+SHFT+$	Applies the Currency format with two decimal places (negative numbers in parentheses).
CTRL+SHFT+%	Applies the Percentage format with no decimal places.
CTRL+SHFT+^	Applies the Exponential number format with two decimal places.
CTRL+SHFT+#	Applies the Date format with the day, month, and year.
CTRL+SHFT+@	Applies the Time format with the hour and minute, and AM or PM.
CTRL+SHFT+!	Applies the Number format with two decimal places, thousands separator, and minus sign (-) for negative values.

CTRL+SHFT+*	Selects the current region around the active cell (the data area enclosed by blank rows and blank columns). In a PivotTable, it selects the entire PivotTable report.
CTRL+SHFT+:	Enters the current time.
CTRL+SHFT+	Copies the value from the cell above the active cell into the cell or the Formula Bar.
CTRL+SHFT+( )	Displays the Insert dialog box to insert blank cells in Microsoft Excel.
CTRL+Minus (-)	Displays the Delete dialog box to delete the selected cells.
CTRL+;	Enters the current date.
CTRL+`	Alternates between displaying cell values and displaying formulas in the worksheet.
CTRL+'	Copies a formula from the cell above the active cell into the cell or the Formula Bar.
CTRL+1	Displays the Format Cells dialog box.
CTRL+2	Applies or removes bold formatting.
CTRL+3	Applies or removes italic formatting.
CTRL+4	Applies or removes underlining in Microsoft Excel.
CTRL+5	Applies or removes strikethrough.
CTRL+6	Alternates between hiding objects, displaying objects, and displaying placeholders for objects.
CTRL+8	Displays or hides the outline symbols.
CTRL+9	Hides the selected rows.
CTRL+0	Hides the selected columns in Microsoft Excel.

CTRL+A   Selects the entire worksheet. If the
                    worksheet contains data, CTRL+A selects the
                    current region. Pressing CTRL+A a second
                    time selects the current region and its
                    summary rows. Pressing CTRL+A a third time
                    selects the entire worksheet. When the
                    insertion point is to the right of a function
                    name in a formula, displays the Function
                    Arguments dialog box. CTRL+SHFT+A inserts
                    the argument names and parentheses when
                    the insertion point is to the right of a
                    function name in a formula.

CTRL+B   Applies or removes bold formatting.

CTRL+C   Copies the selected cells. CTRL+C followed
                    by another CTRL+C displays the Clipboard.

CTRL+D   Uses the Fill Down command to copy the
                    contents and format of the topmost cell of a
                    selected range into the cells below.

CTRL+F   Displays the Find and Replace dialog box,
                    with the Find tab selected. SHFT+F5 also
                    displays this tab, while SHFT+F4 repeats the
                    last Find action. CTRL+SHFT+F opens the
                    Format Cells dialog box with the Font tab
                    selected.

CTRL+G   Displays the Go To dialog box. F5 also
                    displays this dialog box.

CTRL+H   Displays the Find and Replace dialog box,
                    with the Replace tab selected.

CTRL+I   Applies or removes italic formatting in
                    Microsoft Excel.

CTRL+K   Displays the Insert Hyperlink dialog box for
                    new hyperlinks or the Edit Hyperlink dialog
                    box for selected existing hyperlinks.

CTRL+N   Creates a new, blank workbook.

CTRL+O   Displays the Open dialog box to open or find a file. CTRL+SHFT+O selects all cells that contain comments in Microsoft Excel.

CTRL+P   Displays the Print dialog box. CTRL+SHFT+P opens the Format Cells dialog box with the Font tab selected.

CTRL+R   Uses the Fill Right command to copy the contents and format of the leftmost cell of a selected range into the cells to the right.

CTRL+S   Saves the active file with its current file name, location, and file format.

CTRL+T   Displays the Create Table dialog box in Microsoft Excel.

CTRL+U   Applies or removes underlining. CTRL+SHFT+U switches between expanding and collapsing of the formula bar.

CTRL+V   Inserts the contents of the Clipboard at the insertion point and replaces any selection. Available only after you have cut or copied an object, text, or cell contents.

CTRL+W   Closes the selected workbook window.

CTRL+X   Cuts the selected cells.

CTRL+Y   Repeats the last command or action, if possible in Microsoft Excel.

CTRL+Z   Uses the Undo command to reverse the last command or to delete the last entry that you typed. CTRL+SHFT+Z uses the Undo or Redo command to reverse or restore the last automatic correction when AutoCorrect Smart Tags are displayed.

F1	Displays the Microsoft Office Excel Help task pane. CTRL+F1 displays or hides the Ribbon, a component of the Microsoft Office Fluent user interface. ALT+F1 creates a chart of the data in the current range. ALT+SHFT+F1 inserts a new worksheet.
F2	Edits the active cell and positions the insertion point at the end of the cell contents. It also moves the insertion point into the Formula Bar when editing in a cell is turned off. SHFT+F2 adds or edits a cell comment. CTRL+F2 displays the Print Preview window.
F3	Displays the Paste Name dialog box. SHFT+F3 displays the Insert Function dialog box.
F4	Repeats the last command or action, if possible. CTRL+F4 closes the selected workbook window.
F5	Displays the Go To dialog box. CTRL+F5 restores the window size of the selected workbook window in Microsoft Excel.
F6	Switches between the worksheet, Ribbon, task pane, and Zoom controls. In a worksheet that has been split (View menu, Manage This Window, Freeze Panes, Split Window command), F6 includes the split panes when switching between panes and the Ribbon area. SHFT+F6 switches between the worksheet, Zoom controls, task pane, and Ribbon. CTRL+F6 switches to the next workbook window when more than one workbook window is open.

F7   Displays the Spelling dialog box to check
                              spelling in the active worksheet or selected
                              range. CTRL+F7 performs the Move
                              command on the workbook window when
                              it is not maximized. Use the arrow keys to
                              move the window, and when finished press
                              ENTER, or ESC to cancel.

F8   Turns extend mode on or off. In extend
                              mode, Extended Selection appears in the
                              status line, and the arrow keys extend the
                              selection. SHFT+F8 enables you to add a
                              nonadjacent cell or range to a selection of
                              cells by using the arrow keys. CTRL+F8
                              performs the Size command (on the Control
                              menu for the workbook window) when a
                              workbook is not maximized. ALT+F8 displays
                              the Macro dialog box to create, run, edit, or
                              delete a macro.

F9   Calculates all worksheets in all open
                              workbooks. SHFT+F9 calculates the active
                              worksheet in Microsoft Excel. CTRL+ALT+F9
                              calculates all worksheets in all open
                              workbooks, regardless of whether they
                              have changed since the last calculation.
                              CTRL+ALT+SHFT+F9 rechecks dependent
                              formulas, and then calculates all cells in all
                              open workbooks, including cells not marked
                              as needing to be calculated. CTRL+F9
                              minimizes a workbook window to an icon.

F10   Turns key tips on or off. SHFT+F10 displays
                              the shortcut menu for a selected item in
                              Microsoft Excel. ALT+SHFT+F10 displays the
                              menu or message for a smart tag. If more
                              than one smart tag is present, it switches to
                              the next smart tag and displays its menu or
                              message. CTRL+F10 maximizes or restores
                              the selected workbook window.

F11   Creates a chart of the data in the current
                            range. SHFT+F11 inserts a new worksheet.
                            ALT+F11 opens the Microsoft Visual Basic
                            Editor, in which you can create a macro by
                            using Visual Basic for Applications (VBA).

F12   Displays the Save As dialog box.

APPENDIX 2

Chart for business model build project

TABLE A2.1

Activity	Manager	Duration
Visual thinking workshop	CEO	2
Research question definition	ET	1
Definition of outputs	DOM	3
Definition of inputs	COO	3
Define variables, scenarios and sensitivities	CE	4
Data collection	DQM	6
Valuations: income, costs, financials	FD	3
Investment appraisals	FD	1
Build model	MC	3
Run cases, scenarios, sensitivity analysis	MC	1
Make decisions	CEO, ET	2
Prepare deployment plan	ET	2
Total duration (workdays)		**31**

Key:

CE	Chief Economist	DQM	Data Quality Manager
CEO	Chief Executive Officer	ET	Executive Team
COO	Chief Operating Officer	FD	Finance Director
DOM	Director of Marketing	MC	Model Controller

Formula:
G18=SUM(G5:G17) or simply drag down and use the sigma sign under 'Editing'
Use similar method for each of the other columns

Week 1	Week 2	Week 3	Week 4	Week 5
2		3		
1		2	22	
2	1		1	
	3		13	1
	1			2
1	1			2
6	6	7	7	5

APPENDIX 3

Discounted cash flow tables

TABLE A3.1 Rate of discount given as 3 decimal places

Years	1	2	3	4	5	6	7	8
1	990	980	971	962	952	943	935	926
2	980	961	943	925	907	890	873	857
3	971	942	915	889	864	840	816	794
4	961	924	888	855	823	792	763	735
5	951	906	863	822	784	747	713	681
6	942	888	837	790	746	705	667	630
7	933	871	813	760	711	665	623	583
8	923	853	789	731	677	627	582	540
9	914	837	766	703	645	592	544	500
10	905	820	744	676	614	558	508	463
11	896	804	722	650	585	527	475	429
12	887	788	701	625	557	497	444	397
13	879	773	681	601	530	469	415	368
14	870	758	661	577	505	442	388	340
15	861	743	642	555	481	417	362	315
16	853	728	623	534	458	394	339	292
17	844	714	605	513	436	371	317	270

Discount factors are given to 3 decimal places with the decimal point omitted.

Formula: $\dfrac{1}{(1 + i)^n}$ where i = rate of discount and n = number of years

Use the above formula if you need to extend the table's rows or columns

Example of use: The value of £1 in 5 years' time using the discount factor is 3% is £0.86

9	10	11	12	13	14
917	909	901	893	885	877
842	826	812	797	783	769
772	751	731	712	693	675
708	683	659	636	613	592
650	621	593	567	543	519
596	564	535	507	480	456
547	513	482	452	425	400
502	467	434	404	376	351
460	424	391	361	333	308
422	386	352	322	295	270
388	350	317	287	261	237
356	319	286	257	231	208
326	290	258	229	204	182
299	263	232	205	181	160
275	239	209	183	160	140
252	218	188	163	141	123
231	198	170	146	125	108

INDEX

(*italics* indicate a figure or table in the text)

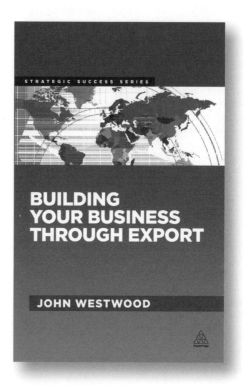

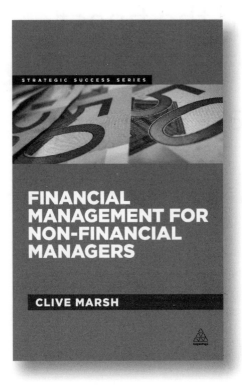

The sharpest minds need the finest advice. **Kogan Page** creates success.

www.koganpage.com